UnBrokable*

IV

The 4th 10 Reasons Why People Go Broke Despite Working

Brad Kong

Disclaimer

These are the full title and subtitle of this book:

__UnBrokable IV:__*
__The 4th 10 Reasons Why__ People Go __Broke__ Despite Working

   I wrote only "*__The 4th 10 Reasons Why Broke__*" on the front cover *intentionally* for rhyme, simplicity and focus.

   The graphic on this book cover is from Edit.org. I use the site to design my covers; it provides book cover templates with its copy-righted images to writers who paid "annual memberships."

   I do have three proofs of my membership to Edit.org, payment receipt for the membership through Paypal and reference address to the image of the site. I am writing this because I received emails regarding my "book cover images" twice; both of which were resolved within a day. I decided to stick to my own or edit.org's images since I cannot keep getting copyright emails. If you have any issue regarding my cover art, feel free to contact me: I will be more than happy to provide the three proofs again.

Also by Brad Kong

UnBrokable* series:

Introduction to UnBrokable*

UnBrokable* I (Chapter 1 to 10)
UnBrokable* II (Chapter 11 to 20)
UnBrokable* III (Chapter 21 to 30)

UnBrokable* Sketch series:

Introduction to UnBrokable* (Chapter 1 to 5)
Intro to UnBrokable* Large Print

UnBrokable* I (Chapter 1 to 10)
UnBrokable* II (Chapter 11 to 20)
UnBrokable* III (Chapter 21 to 30)
UnBrokable* IV (Chapter 31 to 40)
UnBrokable* V (Chapter 41 to 50)
UnBrokable* VI (Chapter 51 to 60)
UnBrokable* VII (Chapter 61 to 70)
UnBrokable* VIII (Chapter 71 to 80)

UnBrokable* (Chapter 1 to 80)

Brad Short Story Collection I:

Robbery at Cyb Knight
How to Get Rid of Ladies
11 Girls I had Loved
Say No To TSLA
3 Ways to Avoid Divorce

15 Ways to Keep Your Teeth Healthy
5 Moments When I Felt Sorry For My Cat
Corn Dog Grandpas
Condo Chronicle
How to Lose 40 Pounds

Brad Short Story Collection II:

15 Things You Didn't Know About Korea
3 Reasons Why We Need to Buy a Home Early
Why Are CDs Super Important?
Say No To TSLA (2nd Edition)
Large Pizza for $5
30 Reasons Why I am Great
3 Reasons Why the Nursing Home filed Bankruptcy

Free books are available all the time!

1. Go to: https://amazon.com/author/bradkong
2. Filter books by "Price Low to High."
3. Download available free books.
4. Read and please leave a rating.

All the books are available free for 5 days every 3 months – read all of them! Grow and enrich your life!

Praise for *UnBrokable*

"This is the best book I have ever read. I am saying this only because Brad is my husband."

-Tsina D,
A housewife and teacher

"I cannot believe my dad wrote this much thick book. He must be a genius."

-Yuna K,
An elementary school student

"I am proud of my son who wrote a book in English."

-Mrs. Jin,
A wealthy woman

"Publishing this book is a celebration itself. Write your name on the next page if you bought this for a gift."

-Brad K,
A philosopher, writer, publisher, book designer and investor

Un*Brokable**

Dear _____

This book is my gift for you.
It has been helpful for me, so I hope it will be
helpful for you as well.
Thank you always.
Sincerely,

From _____

For All the Honest Workers
Struggling Everyday

Foreword

So many books out there from Self-Help and Financial Gurus talk about personal finances in abstract terms. These are folks who make millions selling books telling us what to do. Here is something new and refreshing, however. The author relates his real-life experiences in personal finance. Not only is there a lot of good advice in here, it is an interesting look into someone else's life.

It seems we are at a time in history where everyone is struggling to get ahead. But then again, if we look back in history, it has always been this way. The inflation of today pales to that of the 1970's. The unemployment of a few years ago was nothing like that era, either. What is frustrating for so many is that even "making good money" people are living "paycheck to paycheck" and wondering where the money all went. I know I fell into this trap!

The author illustrates how people go broke even while making a hefty salary, and provides a guide to being "UnBrokable" - a term he has coined. And apparently it works - he retired at 40, not from selling self-help books (like so many Gurus do) but by being careful with money.

There is a lot here to learn from. And it's only just getting started!

Robert P. Bell
Georgia
USA

Mr. Bell is a retired Patent Attorney, self-made millionaire and founder of **Living stingy** blog. He has written in the last 15 years since 2008 and helped tons of people get out of debts and money problems. He is known for his humorous witty but sharp writing style and has influenced myriads of writers and bloggers, including Brad Kong.

Contents

UnBrokable III

UnBrokable IV*

UnBrokable* VII

67. Not Solving Housing Problem Quickly

68. Much on Ceremonies & Anniversaries

69. Not Using Infrastructure Already Built

70. Not Working While Being Wealthy

UnBrokable* VIII

71. Going Too Big

72. Not Being Awake

73. Too Fantasizing Wealth

74. No Long Term Vision

75. Being Deceptive

76. Being On the Wrong Side

77. Not Going Straight to "Profitable or Not"

78. Having Low Self Esteem

79. Not Being Constructive

80. Not Having Enough Room to Breathe

Prologue

Dying poor is a shame, especially in wealthy countries:
It is not about money – it shows how we have lived.
-Brad Kong

This is me sitting on the Ferrari in Miami, FL in 2003 - a rich boy
spending parents' money crazily. Then, I didn't expect I would go
abysmally broke and suffer for a long time.

Hamas from Palestine attacked Israel in October 2023. A
war broke out and over 1,300 people have died so far in the
past week. I am not sure of anti-Zionism, but if I were
Israelis, I wouldn't have tried to expand my territory against
Palestinians. **Technically, the land of current Israel
doesn't have much commercial values – no oil,
agriculture or water resources.** I would try to keep

some lands near Tel Aviv, which is over 10 times bigger than Hong Kong or Singapore, and try to build a new city like Dubai there. I wouldn't have fought over useless lands with poor Palestinians; I would rather let them keep most of it as I need what I need. **The fact that we don't think practically can be a reason to be poor.** *Land used to have "absolute values"* in agricultural societies, but that's an *old concept*, not applicable any more. Also, I wouldn't stick to Jerusalem itself necessarily, only because my ancestors lived there once. The *point* is to obtain new land to settle safely. 90% of Australia or Canada are virtually empty now. I wonder what would Moses do if he governs now – by the time he led the Exodus[1] of the Israelites out of Egypt, North America was not even discovered yet.

Jack Whittaker was a construction businessman in Putnam County, WV – known as the winner of a lottery jackpot of $315 million in the Powerball in 2002. He was a millionaire already with a net worth of $17 M even before winning – in a word, a rich man won a bonanza. Oddly enough, a series of unfortunate events happened to him afterwards. First of all, a guy named Tribble, the boyfriend of Whittaker's granddaughter Brandi, was found dead from drug overdose in Whittaker's home in 2004; three months later, Brandi herself was also found dead at the age of 17; cocaine and methadone were found in her body. Five years later, Bragg, who was Whittaker's daughter and the mother of Brandi, was also found dead in Daniels, WV; the police suspected OD again. Then, Whittaker's home in Bland County, VA, was reported to be on fire in 2016. Finally,

---

[1] 1,400 B.C.

Whittaker himself passed away following a long illness at 72 in 2020: *Why did the luckiest guy in the world pass away "relatively early" after losing all his children?* I am not a Jewish or Muslim, but I turned 50 this year. The best thing I am glad about myself is that I haven't drunk or smoked for life; I have been aware that my body is the most important asset. I am glad that I didn't damage my organs more than now, though my kidneys and teeth are somewhat impaired by drinking sodas for decades.

Han Liu was a Chinese billionaire, the former chairman of Hanlong Group known for mining businesses. His assets were claimed at $6 billion USD by the time he passed away at 49 in 2015. He was convicted of murdering 8 people and running a mafia-style gang for businesses; he was executed by the law enforcement in China. His last words had been viral online: "Life is short; *we don't have to live too tenaciously for more money.* I will have a small store next life and live happily with my family."

The episodes above gave me some lessons: we don't have to work to death, make a lot, spend more and leave a fortune to others; I do not want to *grind* myself to donate more. In *Psychology of money* by Housel, there is a story of a man named Read; he was a janitor for 42 years, made a fortune out of blue-chip stocks, left $8 million to a hospital and passed away. I know a similar case of Groner who worked as a secretary for 43 years, made profit out of the Abbott shares, left $7 million to a college and died. They were honorable. But, seriously, *what's the point?*

What would be the thing they regretted the most? As long as I have enough, I conclude that **the best reward I can give to myself is *working less*.** I may not need a luxury car, but I like to save myself from drudgeries.

Have you ever been a dishwasher before? **If you don't fully agree with this book, it's possible you might not have been broke enough.** I believe a way to be *sufficient* is staying away from the reasons causing poverty. Coincidentally, I was in Chinatown Chicago the other day; it had some Korean shops, which were crowded. It took forever for Korea to be wealthy, but ironically, once its people became rich, I learned they made money out of the fact: *Being prosperous can be a source of income itself.*

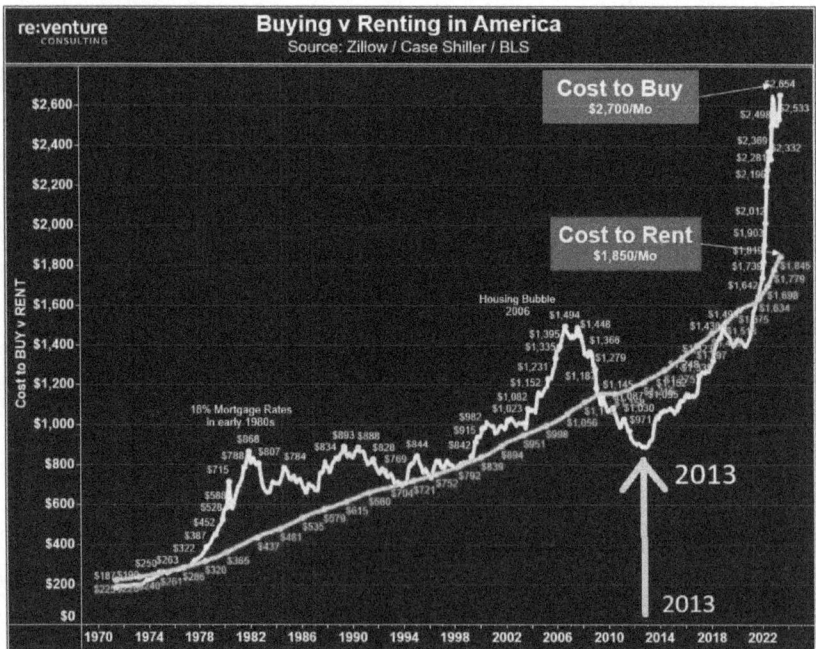

re:venture CONSULTING

Buying v Renting in America
Source: Zillow / Case Shiller / BLS

Cost to Buy $2,700/Mo

Cost to Rent $1,850/Mo

Housing Bubble 2006

18% Mortgage Rates in early 1980s

2013

2013

I bought my home in November, 2013. I didn't know it was the lowest price ever in the 21st century (source from Zillow).

My net worth has increased 8 times in the past decade. I had $80,000 CDs in the bank in 2013: How do I recall it? I bought my condo in full of $60,000[2] that year; my real estate agent asked me to submit proof of funds in advance; I didn't know what to do, so I got a receipt from the ATM and gave it to her. Now I have over a $650,000 portfolio, not including my residence, as of 2023. This growth has probably been from inheritance, investment success, salaries and frugality. But I would say that "not having rent or mortgages" played the most crucial role.

I enjoyed my life until I couldn't. And some of us may not since a recession is looming now. Maybe this book is not for the super-rich, the middle-class or even mildly poor. I was in deep destitution, especially around 2009. My business wasn't doing well as the subprime mortgage crisis broke out; my car was a decade old and horrible mechanics kept overcharging me amid pennilessness; then my daughter was born in 2010. I couldn't waste even a single cent for long, but I was able to manage to buy a small condo thanks to my parents; the only advantage was all the housing prices collapsed due to foreclosures due to the heavy depression. This book is written for those: **Unlucky people who have no idea how to get out of poverty.** The Ferrari photo upfront was taken 20 years ago; then, I had no idea how much trouble I was about to

---

[2] It was low due to the economic depression then.

go through. Now I know being wealthy is a combination of skills, knowledge and *luck*. On the contrary, being broke can happen to anyone any time.

* * *

Charles Bukowski (1920 – 1994) was an American poet considered "the laureate of low-life" in the 1970s; he bought his first house 23 years *later* than me. His net worth was over $4 million by the time he passed away: How did that happen? Bukowski was often considered a drunk loser, but I found out that he and I share a few things in common. First of all, we both started writing after our 40s; both had or have one daughter. We both had worked for low income physical jobs; both inherited some money from parents after becoming middle-aged. Also both were born in foreign countries, originally. But it shows that *Buk* bought his first house with a mortgage at 58 in 1979; I bought my condo in full at 40 in 2013. It took an extra 5 years for him to pay off his mortgage, so he ended up buying his house 23 years later than me: What made him take so long?

It is natural if someone goes broke when he or she does not have a job. But some live poor despite working full-time. More ironically, some live wealthy without having a job: *How?* My mother was initially from a poor family (typical old Koreans) and never had a real job. But she has been in the top class in the country most of her life: What happened? This *UnBrokable** series will be a practical and unorthodox guide to stay away from *brokeness*; we will talk about unique reasons, examples and facts, including my memoir. **Brokeness** (not broke**nn**ess[3]) is a noun meaning **"the characteristic of not having enough money."**

Have you ever been broke before despite having a job? Have you been short in spite of working full-time? People may not get broke automatically, especially in wealthy countries; if some are poor despite working to death, I believe there are reasons. *What makes a person poor?* Why do some still rent an apartment after working 12 hours a day for 30 years? I had witnessed a couple of those closely for 7 years. **UnBrokable*** may not be a word we can find in a dictionary yet as I coined it: **A person who cannot be financially broke;** which can be the opposite of *Les Miserable.* I think there is a big misconception in our lives: If we work hard, we will be rich. Nothing can be further from the truth; *in fact, working longer can make us poorer;* some live painfully by exploiting themselves that way. I am a middle-aged man with a wife and daughter from the Midwest and my American life can be divided into four periods since 1999.

1. Colleges: Cornell and SUNY at Buffalo (1999-2005)
2. Business: Cyb Knight Video Games (2006-2014)
3. Employment: A nursing home (2015-2022)
4. Investor and writer (2022 - current)

Or I can divide the 24 years by jobs:

---

[3] *Broke**nn**ness* means "a condition in which something is badly damaged."

- College banquet (2001 - 2002)
- eBay seller (2003 - 2015)
- Cyb Knight store Owner (2006-2014)
- Nursing home dishwasher (2015-2022)
- Investor and writer (2011-current)

There are other jobs with licenses I prefer not to mention (pharmacy technician and medical coder). Also I have worked for myriads of small jobs since high school: convenience store clerk, bar kitchen helper, military soldier, etc.

* * *

Out of all those jobs, the recent *weekend dishwasher* gave me the inspiration to write *UnBrokable** series. The nursing home I worked at is within walking distance from my home. I had a chance to volunteer to work there one day in 2015; unexpectedly, it brought me a permanent weekend position. Then, I had not done anything for a year after closing out my video game store permanently in 2014. At the end of the work, they suddenly wondered if I could do the job at least every weekend. Now I see the reason why as I asked similar questions to others myself; nursing homes always need employees while no one is excited to work there. Since they suggested a reasonable pay and plenty of free food from the kitchens, I accepted their offer. I had the job only on weekends for six years and on Sunday for a year, close to seven years in total.

I never liked that job since it was physically hard, but I have to admit that it has been helpful. First, I had chances to meet a lot of people I would have not without it; there are types of people doing dishwashing for life. Nothing wrong, but I think I was able to see some reasons why they got stuck: **The reasons for keeping them in chains.** I think I had good chances to take a look at their lives; some were *truly great* guys, though. Secondly, the job had brought me physical strength and weight loss, especially in the beginning. Thirdly, these weekend extra salaries, bonus and free food still helped me build up my savings faster. There could be millions of reasons why people go broke: gambling, addictions, car accidents, etc. **Nonetheless, there are others apparently not doing anything wrong, but always being broke despite working**; many have nothing left after some payments withdrawal at the end of month.

* * *

Do you know when I had the hardest time with money? While I worked at the video game store, my daughter was born in 2010. When a baby is born, parents need more money while physically exhausted. Incidentally, the mortgage bubble burst[4] in 2008 and severe depression came from 2009. I guess that businesses must have a hard time these days as COVID has been with us since 2020. While I had wasted my parents' money only to keep my store open, the only good thing I did was buying a condo in full. Since the economy collapsed in 2008, there had

---

[4] The subprime mortgage crisis.

been plenty of foreclosures, short sales and discounted houses on the market – getting rid of my rent and mortgage for good was the only upside during that era.

After having difficulty with money myself and watching others struggling, I started wondering what really makes a laborer in trouble: **Is there any *practical trap* to make full-timers broke even in wealthy countries?** While working in the nursing home, I saw dishwashers still renting apartments even after *30* years of employment. They occasionally worked *double*, meaning up to 15 hours a day: Where did all their money go? Now, are you ready to jump into 80 chapters with thousands of examples? **All the episodes are either from my life or true events throughout history.** By the time we reach the epilogue, I hope that we can be more mature, knowledgeable and close to wealth.

31

Not Being Unique

Unless we are unique, we are replaceable.
-Brad Kong

There is a comedian named *Hong* in Korea; he is known to be openly gay. In fact, he is the only one there as the country is super conservative. I watched a show and this is what he said once: "It is painful to be the only gay in this nation. Still there is an advantage. **No one can replace my roles.**" He is wealthy and has managed his career well in the last 29 years. Another example of uniqueness may be the actor Peter Dinklage, known as "the dwarf" in the Game *of Thrones* series. First of all, I confess that I have to admire him as a man; it must have been hard for him to apply for acting roles, especially in the beginning. Google shows that his net worth is $25 M, which I believe he deserves, but let me ask a question: Would he be that successful now if he is average height? **Possibly not**; it's probable that no one would have recognized anything from him. He may be short, yet I guess he may not be replaceable in particular roles. It shows that he was casted for the newer *The Hunger Games*, too. I am sure he will keep getting new roles, which is fortunate as most Hollywood performers cannot get employed continuously.

Sungwoo Lee used to be an average Joe working at a department store in Seoul, Korea. But he became a local hero making several headlines on news and has his own Wiki[5] page now. Unusually, he has been a hard core fan of the baseball team "Kansas City Royals." The team managers were astonished that they have a serious fan in Korea and invited him with air tickets in 2014. Incidentally, the team has won a series of important games afterward, which gave him a nickname – victory totem for Royals. Would the Yankees care if they have a

[5] Korean Namu Wiki

fan in Korea? The team has a million fans worldwide and Lee could have been just a drop in the bucket.

I go to Subway for only one menu – veggie patty sandwich, which is better than the "impossible meat" to me. It is made of green beans and tastes like the rice cake in Korea. No other restaurant is selling it. And the day they get rid of it would be the last time I go there since I don't eat other menus. Likewise, the reason why I go to Zupas is because of their crab avocado sandwich: **No one else is selling it, again.** Subway used to have a similar one called "seafood sensation," but they dropped it from menus. I have no choice but to go to these two when I miss them.

I remember I visited Ribfest in Lincoln Park in 2007. It was a year after I opened my video game store and the festival had a PlayStation mobile truck; people played *Uncharted 2* for free in the modified trailer. It had about 20 restaurants under the tents selling ribs. Nonetheless, do you know which vendor sold the largest amount of food? There was only one selling grilled corn on the cob, a popular side dish for barbecue; people were in a long line for the vendor while others didn't seem to have crowds.

* * *

Greene[6] mentioned that a lot of hired soldiers used to be killed by the States which employed them originally in

---

[6] An author.

the Middle Ages; they were fired, imprisoned or even executed after winning battles for the States. They were readily replaceable after all, while many tried to take more power or salary from their employers after winning; many did not realize there are others who can do the same jobs. When I think about it, Jeanne d'Arc[7] was also burnt to death after saving France. Greene wrote a story about an indispensable astrologer in *The 48 Laws of Power*.

Louis XI (1423-1483) was a king in France and had an astrologer in his palace. One day, the foreteller predicted that a lady in the court would die within 8 days and it came true. Louis XI worried that it's either this prophet killed the woman or he has too strong *sorcery* power; the king finally decided to murder him. When the soothsayer arrived in the king's room full of soldiers, Louis XI asked him the final question: "When do you forecast you will die, sorcerer?" He answered, "I will die three days before you die, Sire." The King asked soldiers not to kill the astrologer; actually he provided him with the finest doctors in the country. History shows that the astrologer actually had lived several years longer than the king. By wisdom, he made himself indispensable and saved his life.

I notice that Thai foods are always more expensive than Chinese; usually Chinese lunch specials are close to $8, whereas Thais are over $10 in 2023. Why? Thai restaurants are rarer than Chinese; I don't see other

---

[7] Joan of Arc.

reasons as a Korean. When I think about the ingredients, those should cost about the same for both. **In this logic, the best way for us to make more money is being rare or better yet to be – the only one.** It does not matter for whichever field we work in; we just need to be someone people cannot find anywhere else. In the case of my books, I hope people say I have never seen a book like this. I think that's a success itself by my definition – being distinctive.

In *12 Rules for Life,* Peterson estimated there are about 1.5 million new titles of books published in North America a year, but only 500 of them sell more than 100,000 copies. What do I have to do to make my books outstanding? If my book can get an award, that would be the best-case, but I know it won't happen anytime soon. I concluded I can write more at least for now. I notice that almost 100% of self-helps are less than 600 pages. I can make my book over 700 pages as KDP allows a maximum of 825 pages for paperbacks. It is possible for some readers to look for the thickest self-helps as a lot of novels are over 1,000 pages[8]. This is the sign that there are readers preferring thick books; when they search for self-helps with over 800 pages, only my results may come out. **I thought that is something I can try without spending extra on ad at least for now.**

* * *

---

[8] For example, *the Game of Thrones* is over 5,200 pages for 5 volumes in a collective box.

Certainly, *being unique* matters to be a successful writer. Before publishing this book, I had to choose 3 categories to list it on Amazon. **Some marketing experts recommended listing a book in as rare a category as possible**; they said it is important to make my book #1 in small sub-categories; otherwise, readers do not even notice there is such a book like mine, inundated by so many others. The two of the categories I chose were "Asian study" and "Asian American writers," as *UnBrokable** can be considered an autobiography, too. The Asian population is less than 8% in America, so most writers cannot list in those. The most cardinal feature of an art is uniqueness – the *originality*, which others cannot find anywhere else. I know *UnBrokable** is not exactly literature, but surely an art created by a human, which I hope is differentiating. The first thing I like to hear is, "I have never seen a book like this."

I believe the same thing goes for our lives. In my point of view, a majority of citizens, including Korean trolls, live too boring lives in the traditional ways: finishing school; getting a job; getting married and having *two* kids; mortgage for 30 years, which will be paid off at 75; retirement; death. I thought I will live with a little bit of variation, if it improves my life. For example, I did not want to live in Korea forever or marry only a Korean woman just because I was born there. I stopped having more children after having one since I did not want to spend my life only on supporting a bigger family (human population is bursting, anyway). I bought a decent condo in full, instead of buying a house with a mortgage. **I won't try hard to be different, but decided not to follow conventional ways blindly.**

As you see, there are a few things distinguishing in this book. The first is three-sentence summaries at the end of each chapter, which is a common practice when someone writes a long article *online* in Korea. People are busy and impatient these days and I notice a surprising portion of book buyers are young people. The second is **bold** sentences – I want readers to get points and move on quickly if they are short of time. I have seen only three books do the same so far: *Life force* by Robbins, *Humor, Seriously* by Bagdona and *How to Fail at Almost Everything*[9] by Adams. I am not copying them, but thought it's one way to finish it efficiently. Honestly, some books are nothing but torture without those features.

The third thing is rare examples related to Korean news and culture. Not many books published in America deal with those, especially in self-help books. I think I can list this series in Korean American literature or Korean American memoir as well. The fourth thing is the spaces between paragraphs. I feel suffocating when paragraphs go on endlessly without having a break. Not many authors use one-line space and indentation together between paragraphs. Some people may find them breathable. Frankly, it may not matter whatever it is – just being different is the key. All or nothing. While

---

[9] Only the Korean version of it has bold sentences.

being unique may not guarantee success, being dull may guarantee failure. Being normal may not be a failure, but certainly not a success, either. When we are unique, we gain more control, which puts ourselves in more advantageous positions.

* * *

When I was at the library five years ago, I found a travel diary book accidentally. It was on the shelves in the new release section; new titles are placed there first and moved to the regular sections as they get old. The female author wrote a journal while taking some trips, including cruise travels to caribbean. What was unique about it was she wrote the entire script in cursive handwriting. She took photos, including a porter boy moving their luggages from the ship, and the black boy wore a red uniform looking like a marching band. She wrote explanations on photos by hand as well. The lady writer seemed to be passionate about her life; the book had hundreds of peculiar photos and I truly felt I was on the trip.

The only problem is I have not bumped into it again in the last five years; unfortunately, I do not remember the exact title; I only picked that up at the new release section and skimmed it through once. Probably it has not been a mega hit, so not many people know about it. I checked amazon for "cruise travelog," "Caribbean travels" or "a travel written by hand," but I could not find it. I even checked the entire travel section in our library; it has about four hundred books and I checked one by one the other day. It was not hard actually since I could tell a book without a color photo easily from the spines. Besides, I know the approximate size of the book, so I eliminated too small or giant books. Why am I trying so hard to find it? **It was unique.** I have never seen a book in *handwriting* with that vividness and warmth. I see myriads of travel guides with photos, but even the photos were different in the book – insignificant enough for guides, but cherishable for memories.

In a sense, this is important for other fields, too. We may not have to be distinctive to survive, but we have to be exclusive to be successful. We can make our ends meet somehow even if we live mundanely; we may not be able to earn much that way, though. **We ought to be *irreplaceable* to be eminent**. I am not talking about being excellent; we just need to be a little bit different in positive ways.

* * *

Summary

1. Some societies think being different is bad.
2. Being unique is essential to get rid of a chunk of competitors.
3. If anyone knows about the travel book I mentioned, please let me know the title in the Amazon review of this book!

32

Not Being Persistent

Being persistent is the only superpower in the real world.
-Brad Kong

Jin-myong Kim is a writer who sold over 6 million copies of his novels only in South Korea. In his late essay, he described the importance of continuation: "Aristotle never knew the exact reason to cause ebb tides. These days, even a child knows it's caused by gravitation from the Moon. Humans only needed a lot of time to learn things. We only need to give birth, raise children and continue generations to find out more."

There was a Mexican restaurant called "Taco-Bout-Joy" in Chicagoland. It was one of those inexpensive joints with a quick setup after renovating an old Chinese takeout. In December 2022, this taco place suddenly made several news headlines. The teenage daughter of the owner made a Tik Tok video of her mom waiting for a customer sadly; she said they had not gotten a single customer for days. So myriads of Tik-tokers shared the video and decided to save the business. A long line had formed despite freezing temperatures for weeks; eventually, the mom and daughter were on the Rachael Ray TV show, too.

Lamentably, the mom had a severe injury on her face, so I could see that she must have lived a harsh life. Nonetheless, this chance could have been like a lottery ticket for most ordinary folks.

Later on, I accidentally found out that the restaurant was *permanently* closed out in May 2023, which was only 5 months after the social media frenzy. She explained that there were disputes among owners since the taqueria was owned by two other people, including her aunt. More crucially, she said the place had to be shut down since it faced a "serious" *legal* issue. I assume it could have been a *health inspection failure*; I cannot think of anything else that serious, on top of my head. Frankly, I didn't feel their kitchen was hygienic as I checked more of her videos then. Which is why I am glad I didn't go there to eat, necessarily. I never despise poor people because of lack of money – *I sometimes don't like the reasons for making them broke.* Keeping a restaurant sanitary is not an issue of having more or less money – keeping things clean requires diligence, which requires discipline in life. Moreover, some just don't do things persistently. Keeping a restaurant open for long is extremely hard and some just give up after a few obstacles.

I saw a novel *The Hotel Nantucket* in the bestseller section in the library the other day; the book was only about 300 pages since the 100 pages in the end was a different story. I felt it's a little unusual since I believed thicker books typically sell more; for example, a lot of fantasies by Armentrout are over 600 pages; *the Game of*

Thrones collection is 5,200 pages for 5 books. At home, I found out that Hilderbrand, who wrote the *Nantucket* series, has written over 32 novels, particularly focusing on summer vacation in the Nantucket area since 2002. Then I felt it is understandable – she has accumulated enough fandom in the last 21 years.

If I keep writing, I may be thriving like her after 32 books. The question is "how can I write that many?" My solution was, above all, forgetting about book sales for a while. I figured I need to find *a big subject* I like to think about continuously for decades, which is "poverty" now. I don't think there is a right or wrong theme to think about: literature is not mathematics – no right or wrong manuscripts. I still suppose a small portion of readers are truly interested in "romance in Nantucket town." Finding a specific topic I am particularly absorbed in and going deeper is the key. For now, I like to contemplate reasons for depriving us of monetary stability. After all, we all need to fight against brokeness and survive.

* * *

Making a fortune may not be as important as getting out of destitution slowly. Upgrading our net worth little by little only one way can improve our happiness; even after owning a treasure, we may feel miserable if our savings decrease somehow; even if it's a little, *always going up* matters. Virtually every writer has experience with failure. I am reading *The Alchemist* by Coelho now; he said he wrote it when he was 41 in 1988 and only 2 copies were sold in the first six months; he mentioned he was old enough to be desperate; he made a new contract with another publisher and it started selling in massive quantities a couple of years later; Coelho's net worth is over $500 million USD as of 2023.

There is a book titled *A Time to Kill* by Grisham. He was a lawyer and politician holding a position in the Mississippi House of Representatives. Naturally, I supposed he is a white elite who never had hardship for life, which turned out to be wrong. It shows that he had 1,000 copies of the first novel in the trunk of his car after it was printed in 1989; he tried to give those out for *free* to the libraries, coffee shops or whoever wants it, but had a tough time getting rid of these; he said a close friend helped him clear those out then. Nevertheless, the novel eventually became triumphant and a movie based on it was a hit as well; the net worth of Grisham is over $400 million USD in 2023.

The German philosopher, Arthur Schopenhauer was a known genius in the 19th century. When his masterpiece *The World as Will and Representation* was first published in 1844, it shows only 200 copies were sold in the first year, which made this young professor frustrated. When the American writer, Henry David Thoreau published his first book *A Week on the Concord and Merrimack Rivers* in 1849, records say that less than 300 copies were sold out of 1,000 copies already printed out. Over 700 copies were returned to Thoreau after years and he wrote that, "I have a library of 900 books at home and 700 are written by myself." Even though *Walden* was more commercially successful later on, only 2,200 copies were sold during his lifetime. Now it's considered one of the top five greatest ever written by Americans in this country. **I think being persistent is the key, which can make a normal person exceptional.** No one seems to start victorious at the first try. Failures often don't do things all the way up to the end. And many end up not achieving anything for life as a result.

* * *

Nomadland by Bruder starts with a story about a generous but poor lady named Linda; she has been poor for life and ended up living in a cheap camper at her age of 66. This book ended with describing her ultimate dream – buying a piece of land without having many building code restrictions and building an eco-friendly house called Earthship. In the last Chapter, it reads she actually bought a four acre of barren land near the Mexican border in Arizona with $2,500 ($200 down payment and $200 a month to pay, afterward). I was curious to see what happened after this, so I checked the internet all over.

You know what, though? It seems she ultimately gave up *again*. I understand she must have gotten into a lot of difficulties; it is not cool during the summer in Arizona, to begin with. Still, I suspect that this could be the reason why she has been broke. Only news I found was that she donated the land to a van dwelling organization. After all, her friends and she did not even start the ambitious project. What a waste of all that researches taking up the last 100 pages of the book. I think *actually doing it* and *doing it all the way up to the end* are the sovereignty – **the only superpower in the real world.**

I usually don't go to the novel section in our library. There is a huge room with tons of novels on the first floor. Lately, I went there every day only to check what the best sellers look like. What I found surprising was that there were a lot of authors who I have never heard of, but have written dozens of books. Have you heard of "Eric Gerome Dickey" or "David Sedaris?" I checked their profiles mainly because each has at least fifteen books on the shelves at the library. Eric wrote black romances until 2021 before he passed away of cancer; David has written diary type essays.

No offense, but I did not exactly sense that their books were outstanding. I felt like most people could have written just that much if provided with a pen and paper. There is a reason why I haven't heard of them. But, at the same time, I learned that their books have a surprising amount of reviews on Amazon. This means commercial success of their books and, in fact, both have been millionaires. Here was my final conclusion: They got famous, more because they have *persistently* written large numbers of books; some writers are rich since they wrote excellent books; others are still prosperous since they published so many books in *one field* continuously even though their articles are not quite masterpieces.

When we see a large quantity of books written by an author, we automatically assume that this writer is talented, so he or she must have written so many books. But the other way around is also viable; the writer keeps writing a lot of books, so he or she ends up being known and doing well. In reality, I believe the second case is more common. No one really gets famous as soon as he or she writes only one book. Think of a novelist you like and check Wikipedia for bibliography of the person. Chances are we'll see the creator has written many books before. Have you ever seen an amusing video on Youtube, clicked the channel of it and got surprised by the number of videos in that channel? For example, there is a channel called Alux and it has 1,500 videos in it. For some reasons, YouTube makes it impossible to count the exact number of videos, but I see those YouTubers must have made efforts persistently for long. Book sales can be the same: **Qualities come from quantities.**

When I searched for "Best-selling fiction authors" on Google, Shakespeare came out #1; he sold two billion copies of his books. Yet did you know that he wrote forty two books of poems and plays? Not many authors write that many, even for professionals. The Harry Potter originator, Rowling has written 15 books so far by 2023. I heard most start-up writers give up after 3 books for life. I saw plenty of wordsmiths have only one book on the library shelves.

* * *

Being persistent does not mean being painful. *UnBrokable** is my first series and I thought I could finish six hundred pages if I keep writing four pages a day for five months. I planned to make all my final books at least six hundred pages; I thought thick books could beat the competition as anyone can write a thin book. Also I guessed readers wouldn't feel ripped off when they get a thicker book for the same price. No one wants to spend tons of money on thin prints. I thought that five months is a reasonable frame since some take years to complete a book. I imagined that I could write a book a year – probably spending five months on writing and seven months on reading. We do not have to kill ourselves to be persistent, but just need to repeat the same routine everyday – *taming a drudgery into a habit is the key.* I usually start writing from 7:00 AM till 1:00 PM and found that it's easier than my previous weekend dishwashing job at the nursing home; I am free in the afternoon these days. If this career goes well, writing would be better than owning a business or being employed.

When I worked at the nursing home over the weekends, the management hired temporary workers occasionally since laborers were constantly short in the dining. I heard some temp guys even quit their job within 30 minutes after starting. In general, their food serving was easier than my dishwashing, though. I still remember I saw a fat Latina working reluctantly in the food distribution. I still recall it only because she had the biggest butt I have seen; surprisingly, she disappeared in the middle of work that day; she didn't even complete the 4 hours of morning shift, and ran away, which was shocking. I guess she must have been busy eating, though. I don't think there is a hope for people quitting jobs even before the first day is over.

When people talk about salaries, they tend to talk about the amount of salary a year – **not many talk about how long they can get it.** Again, "persistence" matters and "how long" may be more important than "how much" as people start living longer. Forced early retirement has been a social problem in Korea and people lose jobs from giant corporations early there (commonly laying off in their 40s). In that case, making $100,000 for 10 years is worse than making $70,000 for 30 years. For the same concept, I usually invest my money in dividend stocks and interest bonds, which I hardly sell. I estimated getting $30,000 interest and dividends each year is more valuable than "buy and sell for quick gain" as our lifespans get longer. Besides, "Buying and selling for quick profit" doesn't work well frequently; no one can predict which direction the stock price moves in the short term, after all.

* * *

Summary

1. Perseverance is the only *superpower* in the real world.
2. Poor people tend to give up anything easily.
3. Some persistently eat a lot, but abandon their jobs quickly.

33

Being a Taker

All we have is what we give.
-Brad Kong

Marie Antoinette was the last Queen of France before the French Revolution in the 18th century. She was executed in guillotine for depletion of the national treasury in 1793; she was 37 years old. In other words, she died because she spent too much government money on lavish parties while French people starved. It shows that no one came to her defense or visited her during her prison term – not even her brother who was the King of Austria, then. I thought this could be an example of the consequence selfish takers get: We cannot be arrogant and keep taking from others forever. Those could be the reasons for privation as well, if not for death.

We meet people all the time, but we may not know who we are dealing with, occasionally – our reasons and instincts are not always immaculate. For example, my coworkers from the nursing home must have had no idea I had a large stock portfolio, considering my job[10] there. We can miss opportunities when we act based on

[10] Dishwashing.

assumptions. Even worse is that we can make enemies unexpectedly that way – some enemies may not seem formidable, but we will never know. This could be another reason why some stay indigent. The stories about Ghengis Khan may be well known, but the writer Greene describes it with details in *The 48 Laws of Power*.

Al-Din Muhammad II was the king of the Khwarezmian Empire in the beginning of the 13th century; it had a huge territory covering Turkey, Iran and Afghanistan altogether these days and the capital was Samarkand[11]. This king had a messenger with plenty of gifts from the Mongol empire one day in 1219. Ghengis Khan was a small king as he only invaded and conquered a part of China, then. What this "*small* king" wanted was to open up the Silk Road again and share the profit from trades together with Mongols. Muhammad simply disregarded this offer.

Ghengis tried again. He sent hundreds of camels filled with treasures this time. Unfortunately, an Islamic governor named Inalchik captured this group before it arrived at Samarkand; he killed the leader of the group and *took* all the treasures himself. Ghengis was a patient man; he thought this could be just a mistake. Uncomplainingly, he decided to send another group of caravans filled with treasures one more time. This time, Muhammad II himself killed the leader, took all the treasures and sent back the other Mongols after shaving their heads. Ghengis considered it as an insult and whispered, "Kill them all." **The stupid from**

---

[11] Samarkand is the Valley of Zarafshan River, Uzbekistan now.

Samarkand did not know who they were dealing with.

The Khan from Mongolia attacked Inalchik's province first in 1220; he captured him instantly and killed him by pouring molten silver into his eyes and ears. While Khan's armies were smaller, they attacked efficiently and surrounded the capital city quickly. Muhammad fled, but died while running away on an island near Caspian Sea in 1220; he was 51 years old. Samarkand was fully destroyed and a large portion of its residents were massacred within the next 11 days. What is the lesson? Sometimes, we have to think we may deal with another Khan now. We will never know who we are dealing with by enemies' appearances.

* * *

It seems a lot of people are not sympathetic to livestocks. I understand we raise them to eat; still they are creatures with their own precious lives. It's not like we have the right to kill them *proudly*. I think that attitude can be the biggest threat to the entire humanity in the end. No species can survive that way, not to mention "thrive."

Depending on where we go, international travel could be a total waste of money; this is true especially when we go to underdeveloped countries like Vietnam. I just read a Korean wanderluster's blog and he said street food vendors in Vietnam often do not give him his change back after sales. Maybe I am writing this since I have been tricked the same way; I just don't see there is a point in visiting these after spending huge on air fares; we do not travel to feel ripped off or get close to low lives. Koreans and Americans often forget "what a country with common sense!" we live in; some others are literally corrupted from top to bottom. I don't think it's a mandatorily good idea to visit the poor only because it's cheaper to tour; we may not learn anything positive from the experience.

In 2003, my girlfriend (wife) and I visited a small grocery north of downtown Chicago; it was near the Michigan lake, so probably the town of Edgewater. I bought a couple of ice creams with cash and the change was $0.05. Disgustingly, the Indian or Pakistani clerk, not an old guy, suddenly winked at me and put the nickel back into the drawer. If that happens now, I will demand my change back for sure, but I didn't know what to do 20 years ago. He can be a taker, but it was the most ugly thing a human could do for a nickel; the best thing he could have done was having a tip jar just in case, which is common sense. Personally, I am not interested in taking someone else's changes: **How many years would I live in this life?** There are plenty of ways to make money fairly, anyway. I honestly doubt if these types of people will ever get opulent – nonsense to go to a country full of those with air tickets. I have to admit that I envy travelers who go all over the world sometimes. Notwithstanding, when I spend money, I prefer having cherishable experiences.

* * *

It's said that there are *three* types of people in a profit sense: takers, matchers and givers. Takers are people taking advantage of others mostly. The problem is that others are not fools, either. I suppose many takers usually end up being poor with a low ranked job, according to my experience, especially with dishwashers. Matchers are those who give and receive help equally, which I believe who I am. Givers are those who give more, which I assume my wife is. Some have been nothing but unpleasant takers from me in my perspective. I have seen most of those at working places; they have been badly off and probably will be broke for life.

The nursing home I worked at had about 1,000 senior residents and 1,000 employees; probably 100 of those staff were in the dining department. Throughout the 7 years of the career, I had chances to speak closely with roughly 15 *dishwashers*. First of all, I think it is just a misconception that all the dishwashers are penniless. Surprisingly, many of them actually had decent living, including owning a house outright. I learned 4 guys paid off mortgages on their houses even though they were in their early 50s – three bedroom houses, not like a one-bedroom condo I have. **We even had a Filipino dishwasher[12] lived in a five bedroom upscale house.** He had worked for two dishwashing jobs day and night and his wife was a well-paid nurse; they had one daughter like me.

---

[12] His name was Remi.

Technically, considering the job, I myself have not been in that bad shape as well; I bought my condo in full at 40. Statistically, not many American do that, regardless of their professions – only 25% of citizens in this country own residences "free and clear," while 75% live in apartments or have mortgages. Even among those 25%, not many pay off their home loans completely before 40 like me. To be fair, their houses may be bigger than mine, though. All I can say is, "It's wrong to assume others' financial situations by their jobs." Among the 15 workers above, there were *only two dishwashers* who had lived in solely rental APTS for life: **P**ancho and **E**nrique. They had never been able to reach the point of getting a mortgage from the bank, though both were about 60. And I recall these two were takers, working in a particularly unfair way.

* * *

I was able to work in the morning shifts two years after the start of the job. Virtually, everyone preferred the morning hours, so he could go home early; seniors had priority for the schedule. The morning shift had two different positions for the dishwashers – pots and the dishroom. Whenever I worked with P or E in the morning, they pushed their job to me in a rude way. Both were Mexicans acting similar; I had so many problems with this iniquity in the beginning, but I gave up eventually. I still do not know why they were not afraid of others' anger and resistance. When we *switched* the positions the next day, they were still rude to push their jobs to me the other way around. How would you feel that you had to give them a forced favor, but they don't do the same favor right next day? I felt used foolishly and bursted my anger a few times – these two acted as if nothing happened the day before.

What I hated the most was so-called "half-washing." There were about ten cooks and two dishwashers in the kitchen every weekend morning. There was not a single day the kitchen was closed in the nursing facility. If pot position washes cooking pots and the dishroom washes dishes, everything could have been perfect. Yet, strangely, whenever P and E were in the pot position, they cleaned them only half way through and brought all to the dishroom, so the other dishwasher could finish pots' cleaning. Probably, it could have saved them little effort to rinse all the pots and stack them.[13] They might have had an easier time doing so momentarily. But, in the end, that made the dishroom job double, which made everyone's work double in the kitchen, eventually. I think these two were egocentric, cunning yet idiotic.

The opposite example was a Mexican boy named Omar – too generous. I discerned that he always helped people too much. I always felt sorry for him since he and P are scheduled together during weekdays.[14] I witnessed P crazily take advantage of him one day. The baffling thing was Omar had been much wealthier than this old P. He

---

[13] Pot cleaning steps are washing, rinsing and stacking; these two notoriously brought pots to the dishroom only after washing.
[14] I had been scheduled with P on weekends.

was only 28, the first child out of five in his family, living in his parents' house then. I confirmed he had saved over $80,000 cash out of the 10 years of work though a certain amount out of his income had gone to aid his parents.

Another example, similar to Omar, was Hector. He had been a great helper to me and had only one child like me. He was about 50 years old and owned a three bedroom house *outright* after his mortgage paid off perfectly. Interestingly, all these four were Mexicans (P, E, Omar and Hector); all spoke Spanish fluently.

After all, P and E continuously had betrayed "mutual help rules" all the way up until the day I resigned. In particular, P forced and demanded help, but never helped others unless it is a woman who he can approach with sexual intention. I had complained about it to management several times, but nothing ever changed. I even tried to change my job to a waiter, but it did not work out for any visible ground. Yet I still deduce this could have been the reason why P and E were broke as hell for life, while Omar and Hector weren't. FYI, the nursing home filed bankruptcy as well with $110 million debt in June, 2023. That was a year after I quit the job.

* * *

Summary

1. Being a taker only makes us penniless.
2. Others are not fools.

3. We don't have to be givers, but I think we must be matchers at least to get loaded.

34

Stuck in a Low Paying Job

Too much comfort can kill us.
-Brad Kong

The Four Agreements by Ruiz explains that our education can be a process of domestication: "Human domestication is so strong that, at a certain point in our lives, we no longer need anyone to domesticate us. We don't need parents or schools. We are so well trained to be our *own* domesticators; we are auto-domesticated animals." I think the old dishwashers at the nursing home, willing to continue *low*-paying but hard jobs, may be **overly domesticated** — taming themselves not getting out of the hard jobs. It's horrible if someone discourages us from moving forward to better jobs; sometimes, we do it to ourselves voluntarily.

Being *lazy for long* is not being persistent. Some work for the same job for decades, even though they know it's not a good one; they just do not want to change things. Often, they make all sorts of excuses for why they should stay in their current jobs – occasionally, some of us are too tired to make any change at all. **I think it is important not to put ourselves in a situation where we must**

accept a bad job, to begin with. I used to feel sorry for those Mexicans who do dishwashing for 30 years since they have five kids to feed; having too many kids is not mandatory for anyone, though; no one is given such an obligation, to begin with.

When we make such a life decision, first of all, I think we have to see if that's what we really want. Then, we need to check if that's beneficial. If it's disadvantageous, at least, we have to estimate how bad it is. I know some men running away from their family after having 8 kids with their wives; one of them was the father of president Lula in Brazil. Some men just don't think. **Ultimately, I ended up believing caring about ourselves profits others the most.**

"Humans are not interested in minimizing risks. Unless there is a limitation, people tend to choose an adventurous life," said the Canadian psychologist Peterson in *12 Rules for Life*. People may not like to be in too much danger; they do not like to have too much boredom, either. The author took an example of skateboarding; it is not as dangerous as skydiving, yet not as safe as walking. People tend to *enjoy* a bit of *risk*, which is why casinos and stock markets are crowded.

As soon as I read it, I realized why I had bought PBI stock a few times after the big sell-off and sold it immediately with trivial profits; I assumed I had been enjoying risks. As I explained, PBI used to give me a headache for four years, but I was able to sell all my 6,500

55

shares with +$20,000 profit in January 2021; I still appreciate the WSB on Reddit for pumping up the price for a couple of days. Before 2021, I had the 6,500 shares of PBI for $10 average purchase price; the price jumped up to $13 only for a couple of days in January 2021, when I sold all with profit. Even after that, I had traded PBI on and off while it was under $4. One time, I bought 250 shares of PBI with $3 average purchase price. I must have thought this was an affordable risk and probably enjoyed the trading; $3 was much cheaper than $10. It has given out a 5% dividend a year anyway, so I did not think I would lose much money.

I guess the same thing goes for the tourism industry as well. When I checked the world tourism rankings on Wiki, I noticed that way more people visit the U. S. than Mexico or Canada. To foreigners, Mexico can be too dangerous a country to visit; I have seen photos of the corpses killed by drug mafias; some were hanged by highway signs; there is no way I can visit there. On the contrary, Canada seems to be too boring despite the outdoor scenery. I think America is not extremely dangerous or too boring.

* * *

There are millions of adults wasting lives by working without meaning; they tend to be old, who are married with their habits; they occasionally work in the same job for decades. In a sense, they go against human instincts, which is averse to boredom. They may or may not be wealthy, but here is one thing to be informed; old employees tend to get paid less than newcomers, according to my experience. **There are not many companies paying their *current* employees more than new ones *voluntarily*;** often, current employees need to demand or fight for the same wage rate newcomers get. In many cases, it's less profitable to work for the same company for long, even though it's ok that we stay in the same field; employers never overfeed the fish they already caught.

Today I visited a huge Indian supermarket for the first time. I had been to Indian groceries before, but they were not ample. As soon as I entered the place, I heard Indian music in the background. Every worker and customer was Indian; apparently, it seems they were surprised to see me. They sold religious statues as well. Unexpectedly, these were elephant goddesses named Ganesha; these could have been Jesus in Mexican or Buddhas in Vietnamese markets. I did not know Indians make so many food products with their own brands[15]. It was a unique experience for 30 minutes – *something refreshing doesn't have to be expensive.*

Some get stuck in their old jobs since it's too comfortable; some of them will find reasons to stay, even though it's not beneficial to keep working there. When I was employed at the nursing home, a couple of dishwashers, working there for 30 years, didn't even try to be a cook. Eventually, I felt **they turned themselves into people who do not know how to do anything**

---

[15] For example, Swad.

else. Coincidentally, I remember these two were quite egotistical and unpleasant human beings I have seen. **To get out of detrimental destinies, my suggestion is to have a habit of always trying something *new*.** It doesn't have to be an expensive thing like visiting a new foreign country. In fact, international travels can bring us the same *repetitive* experiences: waiting at somewhat resembling airports, boarding on the same airplanes probably either from Boeing or Airbus, sleeping at the similar Marriott chains somewhere, etc.

I suggest we can start by eating at a different restaurant, as an example. Today, I tried a new Indian menu (not remembering the name of) at the Mumbai cafe; it cost me only $7. I will try the new Indian egg place[16] next time. On the way back, I found a boat renting for $12 an hour in a pond next to a high school. Maybe I will try that with my daughter next time. Always **try** something new **at least once**, especially if it doesn't cost much. This habit may get us out of old but less-paying occupations as well.

* * *

Hardship does not always grow us; it can crush us or make us exhausted, too. To me, the best life strategy is not to create any hardship, to begin with. The second best would be figuring out and removing the reasons which brought us in a hard situation, if we already created one. Changing a career takes energy and courage. I have changed my job about six times in the last fifteen years:

---

[16] EggHolic.

an eBay seller, game store owner, weekend dishwasher, medical coder, investor and writer. Some of these have been extreme changes. I think this has been possible virtually because I have lived like a single; gratefully, my wife has taken care of my daughter mostly. My daughter and I have lived fantastic lives based on my wife's sacrifice, frankly. In my opinion, there are two major reasons why people cannot change bad jobs – *being too comfortable with them* or *being too tired to make a change.*

People assume that being comfortable may happen only in employment. However, I have observed it happened a lot among small business owners, too. Even if businesses don't make profits, some owners stay forever. **In this case, it is not even a low income, but actually a loss for those owners.** Still, except for the money loss, the life of a small store owner is often fantastic. I believe that is the actual reason why they remain endlessly, according to my experience, though they may give you different reasons. I have been a business owner and employee, but the only job I still keep is the investor – managing a $650,000 portfolio including stocks, bonds and ETFs. Why? **In a cost sense, an investment job is totally different from the other two.**

Simply, owning a store or even working at a nursing home cost me money. It is easy to understand why owning a store costs money upfront: rent, utility, credit card machine charges, employee salary, etc. Oddly, keeping a job costs us money, too: transportations for commuting, nice clothes, haircuts, lunch, etc. Nevertheless, managing an investment has not literally cost me anything so far – **it has not cost money to own stocks**[17]. When I had the video game store, I had to pay about $1,200 rent a month for 8 years by 2014 – a 900 sf space in a Chicago suburb. The total rent had been over $120,000 for 8 years. Plus, I had to pay at least $100 electricity and $50 credit card terminal charges a month. I cannot remember all, but there were numerous other expenses: ADT security charge, license renewal fees from the village, tag fees for fire extinguishers, etc. So, I would say owning the business cost me at least $2,000 a month then.

Business had been good sometimes, but not lucrative mostly during the 8 years. Worsely, I had so many bad months particularly after 2010, as economic depression came after the mortgage bubble burst in 2007. I recall I had lost $1,000 a month in the last 6 months of the 8 years. Nonetheless, I am glad I was able to close it in 2014 before COVID came in 2019. Yet I noticed that some of my business neighbors keep their businesses open forever despite obvious losses. I do not believe they made fortunes while I was in trouble. They usually get money from somewhere (parents, relatives, credit card company, etc) and sustain. The most common excuse would be something like, "Well, more people will know us when we stay longer." They might think they are survivors and I am a loser since my business was closed out: **Often, the other way around is true.** I would have stayed if there

---

[17] When we sell stocks for profit, we have to pay tax. Selling is an option. We can just keep them without selling them.

was no ownership cost as in stock portfolios, but I couldn't continue having inevitable business losses.

* * *

Conclusively, I think there are a couple of true reasons when a business stays for good despite prolonged loss. One is attachment; owners love the businesses they created. The other, which is more harmful, is the cozy life as a business owner. When we own a store, there is no boss there. In my store, customers did not come all the time, so my life was restful. When I worked at a nursing home, I could not even take a break for 10 minutes peacefully except lunch hours[18]. There was a short sous chef notorious for over-concerning. Once, he was looking for me everywhere since I went for a break 5 minutes earlier. I guess he was one of the major reasons why I quit the job. Dishwashing is toiling by nature; most people do not have any room to think about career change at the end of the day.

Notwithstanding, when I think about it, I think we can also use our natural laziness to work in our favor. Once we are settled with good habits, we can kick out any new bad habit this way, too: "It's annoying. I am tired. I do not want to try any new bad things." Some said they made a bonanza out of Bitcoins. In my opinion, it is recent, but can be fraud, too. **I can simply disregard the temptation since I am too fatigued to try new**

---

[18] Luckily, we had a one-hour lunch time. They removed two of the 15-minute breaks and combined them to the 30 minute-lunch time.

investments. I watched some people drowning to death after trying scuba diving in narrow caves. Some die by skydiving. That will not happen to me since I am sapping to try new adventures already.

* * *

Summary

1. Some people make less money since they don't want to change things, including vocations.
2. We all need energy and courage to change careers.
3. We can use laziness not to try something new but risky.

35

Not Minding Your Own Business

Nosey people never do their jobs very well.
-Brad Kong

An irony in our lives is that people who don't need to do a certain thing do it more. For example, it is possible that people who read this book are mostly those who don't have to worry about money. Fat people who don't have to eat often devour more. Obese people having heart attacks go to steak houses more than the skinny. A father with eight kids meets other women continually like Gosselin. Yet a large number of single guys never meet a woman to breed. A single mother with three kids got pregnant twice more like one of my ex-coworker. Yet some single women never have a baby for life (which is fine). Rich people save more and poor people spend more – the rich get richer and the poor get poorer, as a result.

I strongly believe that spending time on being jealous is the biggest waste in our lives; sometimes, this happens nationwide. One French guy on a Korean TV show admitted that Frenchs tend to be more envious than others in general. He said that Americans may dream of owning a nice car in the future when they see a rich man driving a luxury car –

Frenchs would want to get the rich out of the car and force him to walk together. I believe him since France seems to have had more revolutions led by the public in her history; a lot of Kings and Queens killed by guillotines, including Louis XVI and Antoinette. But, at the same time, did you notice that France has conquered smaller territory, compared with its neighbors during the age of colonialism? For example, England had built an empire once covering the USA, Canada, Australia, New Zealand, India, etc. The west neighbor of France is Spain, which was once governing the oceans, and Spanish is still spoken throughout Latin America. After all, what does France have now? No one really speaks French except a small portion of African countries, not far from France.

Why is this happening despite the fact that France has enough ocean sides? Is it possible that French people might have wasted more of their energy and time on being jealous than their neighbors? To be fair, Germany, which didn't acquire many colonies, has very little of an oceanside along its borderline. I am afraid that Koreans are closer to Frenchs than other Europeans; I am Korean and know many of us confess that we have a character of big envies, which could be why those smart people have been stuck in the tiny peninsula for 5,000 years. **In a profit sense, this could be the reason why some are poor while working hard.**

* * *

The Canadian psychologist, Peterson once said, "If you are not the leading actor in your own play, probably you are taking a role in others' plays." The roles others may give us will be mundane – they will never give us the best parts to us in their own plays. Which is why it's important to be the main actor in our own lives; we need to protect ourselves from being nugatory. He also mentioned things about Paranoia in his book; a *paranoiac* assume there are a group of observers thinking about him or her all the time and try to hurt them. Here is good news, though; I don't think there is anyone thinking about us all the time; everyone lives in his or her own body and needs to survive; it is like concerning others' driving while they drive their own cars. We all worry about others' eyes to some extent, but there is no actual need for it.

Losers never get lives in general; their lives are often pointless and boring; commonly, they have nothing exciting or profitable going on. As a result, **they tend to concern others' lives more.** Even on a Korean message board, they never write even a single post on their own; what they do mostly is replying nasty comments on others posts – meaningless negative comments. Keeping losers nearby is harmful. Don't make them part of your family by marriage or have a too close relationship anyhow. Mind our own business *is supposed to* be the easiest in the world. However, it seems it's the hardest for some; this habit of focusing on ourselves humbly requires some discipline. Yet it's worth it since it can prevent divorce or other inharmonies while providing freedom to others. Any conflict, especially with our own family, can cause financial damage, too; alternatively, we can have some distance from them. Regardless, when we shut up and do our jobs modestly, everyone can be happy; he or she may like us, or won't hate us, at least.

* * *

Sometimes, I go to downtown Chicago only to walk around. I do that on my scooter occasionally. I had a kick scooter from Razor, which was about $80 from Amazon. Originally, my wife bought a small scooter for my daughter in 2015. Then, it broke somehow and she bought a bigger version for an adult. Still, you know what, though? I found that the big one has been more than a toy. After riding it for 30 miles one day, I realize that it can be a practical tool of transportation. I tried to walk around for a long distance at least one day a week. The scooter is foldable, so it does not take up a lot of space on a bus or subway. I always put it in the shoe closet at home. Now it is springtime and I know it's not very long in Chicagoland.

I usually go to Chicago by Pace 600. The bus is only $2 one way and I can pay for it with a Ventra card, which looks like a credit card. We can add money on it online or at vending machines at the station and use it for both bus and subway everywhere. It is about 3 miles from the bus terminal to my home. There used to be Pace 608 connecting these, but it was suspended after COVID came in 2020. I usually walk or ride my kick scooter to home, which is more exercise, after all. There is a Target on the way, so I usually shop a little bit, put items in my backpack before arriving at home.

It was 8:00 PM when I came back from Chicago yesterday. My wife was at home checking her iPhone in the living room. When I was eating the leftover Chipotle veggie bowl, she started talking about news everywhere: UIUC civil engineering school ranked #1 in the nation, UIUC is considered a public Ivy League, etc, which was annoying. She graduated from UIUC music twelve years ago and does not have a *real* job now. What is the point for all these? I wish she would listen to my problem instead, so she can get more money from me. My talking was easily cut off by her pointless news. **I hate these people concerning something else other than their own impending issues.** As a result, they never do their own work well.

Then, I was waiting for a phone call from the unemployment benefit agency. They sent me a letter saying that they want to interview me one more time for my benefit. I don't care what others do; I was worrying about my own interview and planning to pass it nicely. FYI, unemployment benefits are not necessarily for the poor. If we have a job for more than 18 months and lose it by some misfortunes we cannot control, we are eligible for 26 weeks; anyone can get it, even if he or she is rich, technically. Citizens can get checks from $200 a week, but no more than $400 even if they have a large family to support, which means the amount is not very significant, to begin with. And the period is 26 weeks at the longest until we find a new job. It is not like Snap cards renewable every year – just a payment of 26-weeks once in our lifetime and that is it. If the same thing happens again, we may theoretically get it again, but less likely that happens with long interval restrictions.

In my case, I was supposed to get $302 a week since I have only one child to support. We can legally get it even if we have savings or investment incomes. The rule is that we should not be hired during the 26 weeks, which the agency checks thoroughly. And the causes for being unemployed should be beyond our control, like getting laid off. After closing my video game business in 2014, I took about a 13 month break. It was nice – one of the happiest eras in my life. I bought my condo in 2013, so I didn't have any rent to pay. I remember my association fee was $290 a month then, so I did not have any heavy obligation. My daughter was 4 years old, but she and my wife were overseas to take care of my ill mother-in-law. Admittedly, my rest was based on my wife's sacrifice.

One day, my wife suggested that I should get a job over the phone. I was a little bored after resting for a year, too. She used to work for "home elderly care" when she was in graduate school. She strongly suggested some similar jobs since nursing homes have occupations available *all the time*. Later, I happened to watch YouTube videos of a Bhuddist monk in Korea. A devotee asked what kind of job he needed to get and the monk answered that he should get any for now and move to a better one later. I filled out an application online that day; I had been a *dishwasher* before both in America and Korea. I had the job interview only for 5 minutes the next day and got it immediately.

The work was fine in the beginning. I was happy to get a slightly higher rate ($11.04 an hour) than others in 2015. Everyone welcomed me, quality meals were free and they gave me a lot of food to take out after work; I remember I didn't have to go to the supermarket even for months. But the problem was the "transferring" to a better department. I ended up working for the organization for almost seven years. My original plan was to slog as a dishwasher for a couple of years and transfer to a better job, eventually. But all the managers blocked me from going to a better position together. These blockings were caused by a combination of bad luck, worse timing and selfishness of managers. Nonetheless, I think I did my best to try to get out of the situation – **passing two exams of medical coder and pharmacy technician by self-study.** I did *what I had to do*, so I don't have any regrets now. Besides, I started making a noticeable amount of dividend incomes out of my portfolio from 2020 since I spent a lot of time reading about investments.

* * *

Finally, I decided to quit the job at the nursing home when a new company Morrison took over the dining department in 2022; it took over only the dining, but nothing else in the huge facility. I had a letter from the CEO stating that the nursing home's management of restaurants would be over by March 2022 and I did not have the right to argue about it. Later on, I got info about *unemployment benefits* from the human resources. That is how I processed the steps to get $604 benefits by April, 2022. But the problem was that IDES[19] contacted the dining staff and asked how I would stop working there: these stupid chefs answered I quit the job *voluntarily*, which was not the ground for benefits. I did not quit the job on my own; **I was pushed out,** even though I didn't resist to stay, which was supposed to be a solid ground for getting benefits.

Before I stopped working, I suggested transferring myself to Morrison twice, but it was declined for no apparent reasons. Maybe those managers knew that I was not happy with the dining for long (no one was). When I suggested the second time, they said the transfer period was already over and I had to fill out a new application as a *newcomer*; they said they would give a lower hourly rate – absurd since everyone knew I had been there for seven years. The last thing I did before quitting was applying for the transportation department in the nursing home. Even though I have a driver's license with an immaculate record, they did not choose me in the final stage with no explanation. I could not do the dishwashing job forever. They acted as if they wanted me to do only the job for good – even at a lower rate.

It had a short Mexican sous chef everyone did not like in the kitchen. He was the major reason I tried to move out of the dining, originally. It seems he was not helpful to me even after I stopped working there since I believe he was the

---

[19] Illinois Department of Employment Security.

one answering the IDES incorrectly. First of all, the nursing home did not have to answer anything at all, to begin with. The policy is if there is no reply for 10 days, IDES doesn't bother to verify the unemployment reason repeatedly. IDES had seven years of my wage record already and I believe they basically tried to help people in misfortune. That sous chef never helped me when I worked there and still was a pain for benefits outside. Secondly, he should have answered correctly, at least. Unlike me, most did not save letters from the CEO. These chefs were all hired by Morrison years ago and started their careers in the nursing home as outsourcers. As a result, they do not know what exactly happened to which member in the kitchen; there are over thirty cooks and dishwashers there. When someone disappeared, they seemed to assume it was voluntary quitting, which had been common, in fact. I am glad I saved the CEO letter for proof of my forced resignation.

I wish my wife had a chance to talk all about these with me. She checks the internet news too often and knows something we really do not have to know. We had heavy rain today and I got three Tornado warnings via my smartphone, which is unusual. I was going to check the exact location of the storms, but my wife suddenly asked if I remembered the sports team mascot of my college while she was reading a novel. I do not know what is wrong with her, but I could see why she is unemployed. Employers need members who can focus on their jobs without concerning irrelevant things.

Have you ever been disgusted at yourself since you know too much about entertainment? I have. In 1999, I studied at the language school in Cornell and tried to apply for graduate schools. When I was with my girlfriend, who is my wife now, suddenly the music "American woman" came out from the theater speakers. She said, "It's from *American Beauty*." I knew it was from *Austin Powers*. Then, all of sudden, I got upset at myself, 'Why do I even know this? Without getting accepted by any graduate school?' Both movies were released that year. FYI, **my unemployment benefit was canceled finally** since IDES decided that I was not qualified. Incidentally, the nursing home also filed bankruptcy in June 2023.

* * *

Summary

1. Some stay poor since they are too concerned about others' businesses.
2. Minding only our own things needs discipline.
3. Losers care more about celebrities.

36

Living in a too Big or Old House

A car and house are two things putting us in pain only because we own them. -Brad Kong

The book *48 Laws of Power* starts with a story of Nicolas Fouquet, who was the Superintendent of Finances in France under the Sun King Louis XIV in the 1650s. It shows Fouquet had a glittering career initially and acquired an enormous amount of wealth in the beginning; he was also known for his extravagant spending style and frequently throwing lavish parties. At that time, he owned a magnificent chateau called "Vaux-le-Vicomte"; it was so luxurious that Louis XIV got an inspiration and had the same architects build the Palace of Versailles for himself later on.

It says Fouquet was expected to be a prime minister after the former PM, Mazarin, passed away in 1661. Instead, King Louis just eliminated the position of PM itself for any reason. So Fouquet decided to throw a big party for the king to show his royalty, with an excuse to celebrate the completion of his castle, *Vicomte*. He invited 6,000 people to throw a housewarming party for the chateau, but his real intention was to flatter the king and give him an impressive time. All the royal celebrities in France gathered at that party and everything seemed to be pleasant.

Then, do you know what happened, though? Out of the blue, Fouquet was arrested two weeks later and got a life sentence for stealing from the government treasury; history says that it was not practically a fair accusation for Fouquet. Nonetheless, he spent 15 years in solitary confinement before he died in the obsolete Pyrenees mountain prison. Technically, I assume it's more than just jealousy in this case. Fouquet overwhelmed then 22-year-old Louis XIV with all of his treasures and power and made the king worry his power looked smaller than Fouquet.

To begin with, I don't think it's ever a good idea to make anyone jealous. Jealousy equals anger – the fact that *someone* is angry at us will not be helpful anyhow. As you see, people can even go to prison or be dead if that *someone* is our superior. *The 48 Laws of Power* started with a chapter titled "Never *outshine* your master," which I understood as "Do not make anyone jealous, especially our bosses." In my opinion, one way to offend others unnoticeably is to buy a needlessly big house or luxury car for ourselves; these two not only cost us money, yet bring all sorts of problems, including unwanted attention. **Houses and cars require constant care, which will be headaches in the end**; getting anger anonymously from everywhere will be a bonus.

These are a couple of stories I found about jealousy online accidentally. When cannibals, who eat the flesh of other humans, in a remote Pacific island need to sacrifice someone in their village during the famine, it says that they usually choose a guy with a beautiful wife, first. During the emergence of communism in the early 20th century, poor peasants killed rich farmers before others in Russia and China; it was not all about the unfair social systems; it was about human psychology, too. In my logic, it's not a fantastic idea to drive a luxury car, especially to work – **never show it to your directors or customers if you need to get paid by them.** In fact, I think sages never show their money to anyone and know how to live simply. I am honestly happy with my condo – 850 sf is enough for my family of three. I feel comfortable when I don't drain a lot of cash. *Being frugal is an extra layer of security to protect my family.*

* * *

Bill Issued	08/18/2023	$25.69
Bill Issued	07/20/2023	$27.37
Bill Issued	06/20/2023	$23.61

My recent electric bills – *big residences were created to keep us poor.*

I believe our savings start from lowering *electricity* bills as they're *recurring charges* - there has been *no month* I didn't pay for it. The other day, a Korean guy complained that he spent over $400 on electricity a month over the summer – due to air-conditioning. It's not like I didn't use it; my condo is facing north, which makes the unit cooler and I live in a smaller condo while he lives in a *bigger* house. I believe he lives in TX or CA, while I live in chilly IL. Making others envious by showing off a big house can put us in ruination. When people have enough money, I guess the true qualities of them come out. Some may start a decent hobby like writing. Others may spend some of it on new vehicles or move to larger houses. The worst can be spending all of it on drugs or even getting into extra debt to do so; as a result, a few actually become poorer only because they acquired some dough in hand.

I usually focus on eliminating bad stocks from my investment portfolio. In stock investing, some focus on buying good stocks, which I used to. Now I have 70 company stocks and 38 company bonds, as of 2023; the portfolio has grown from $100 in 2011 to $540,000 in 2023. While a lot of my stocks are fine, I think about 20 company stocks have given me a headache. Experts are said to expect a recession soon; I think it's more wise to get rid of bad apples now than look for better companies to buy; all the stock prices may drop gradually, as we get into a depression. – the same thing goes for a house.

People may feel more comfortable when they walk on quiet back streets than the bright loud main streets; I feel more relaxed when I sit in a nameless park than crowded theme park; people may feel more restful when they live in a moderate house without debt than a luxurious one with a mortgage. **We often don't realize how mental comfort is overriding**; many have forgotten to live for themselves, instead of living to show off to others. Many don't recognize the beauty of simple living; some just go for a bigger one, even with a huge amount of debt.

* * *

When it comes to a physical problem in buildings, roof leaks always have made me crazy; I am serious that I get a panic attack from it. It is supposed to be an easy thing to fix since we are living in the 21st century now. But, for some reasons, I have never had luck with roof repairs. No matter how much I tried, roof leaks had kept happening to me for a long time – I ended up having a phobia.

While I am not a complaining type, my wife always complains about temperatures. Now it is May and it was over 80 F in Chicagoland today; I was happy since I did not feel freezing any more. But she got upset since it was too hot this morning; she always raises the furnace up to 75 F even in the spring since it is freezing for her – all she does is complain. It is sad to see a happy young girl turn into a grumbling grandma as I met her 24 years ago. And who made her this way? Herself. No one asked her not to get a good job. Whenever I mention a job, she always makes an excuse that she cannot do anything since she has a child: How many kids do we have? One. Humans cannot have less than one. I got a feeling that she will keep complaining, making excuses and being needy until death – no cure for these types of people.

I started my business at a large stirp mall in 2006. It was an old but colossal plaza, but I rented only 900 sf, so we occupied less than 1% of the property. We were located in the middle of the complex and it had an ample parking lot. It was great that we had a stop sign right in front of the store, so people could see us whenever they made a stop before passing by. But, unfortunately, the space had the roof leaks all along for 8 years. It had a ceiling with tiles under the main roof, which was nice since it cut out the large amount of air space in half; it blocked cold air and noise from the roof, too. I saved a lot of money for heating and cooling since we only needed to take care of the space below the ceiling, excluding the one from the ceiling to roof. But I noticed that the ceiling tiles always got wet whenever it rained in the first year.

Actually, the very first roof leak started from the air-con located on the middle of the roof in the store. I called the landlord and he sent us a couple of roof guys hired for that plaza and the issue seemed to be gone immediately. They mentioned that some storm seemed to move the air-con unit; it was ok for a while. The major roof leak had been at the north east corner of my store. I started repairing that by buying a lot of ceiling tiles from Home Depot and replacing them in the beginning. After doing that for a couple years, I bought a caulk gun and sealants one day. I climbed by a ladder, opened the sealing tile and went up to the roof to seal up leaking spots myself. When I think about it now, it was dangerous since the distance from ceiling to roof was over 6 feet. I barely stood on top of the ladder. Whenever I complained, they said they will do a roof renovation for the entire plaza soon.

I recall they did a major roof construction in 2008, but, weirdly, things did not get better. **I think I started going crazy and having a phobia from that point.** It took almost a year to finish the assembly in 2009. There was one time they made a mistake pouring a bucket of water on the roof and I saw a new water leak coming at a totally new spot. How hard is it to fix a roof leak? I live in

America in the 21st century. I started to wonder how some hotels can have swimming pools on the rooftop or in the middle of buildings. They explained that they did not work on that particular spot yet. After finally finishing the total renovation, I thought that I would never see a roof leak again. How hard could it be as humans were on the Moon sixty years ago? It was just a matter of money for new construction, right? Wrong! Soon I started having different roof leak problems.

* * *

The landlord suddenly sent a new air-con guy to our store for check up and I found the roof around our air-con started leaking; that was in the middle of the store, not the corner as before. The stupid landlord said so many different people touched the air-con units, so that caused those leaks; he said he found a "quality" technician somewhere and everyone should use him mandatorily. It was $65 for filter change and check up service, so I did not expect any trouble. Yet it seems these "recommended" technicians started hiring "not very reliable looking" subcontractors soon. And right after they touched the air-con, I started seeing water marks around the air-con on the ceiling again. **I went literally crazy:** How can I get out of these leaking problems? When they came again, I asked them not to touch our unit ever again – Not only for money, it was psychologically *aggravating*.

I ended up solving the problem completely by not owning a business there. I didn't make a huge amount of profit out of the business, anyway. I made that decision in 2012 and our lease contract was over in 2014 – I did not renew the store lease. After closing out my store, I saw the big Polish supermarket in that plaza had a massive roof leak around their door area. I was more than relieved that I did not have anything there any more.

* * *

It seemed owning a small condo solved my problem entirely. Still, unluckily, I had a couple of leak problems around the chimney area in my condo in 2015. I called the association and they sent technicians a couple of times and everything looks fine after that. I live on the top floor of our residential building. I still could not believe the roof leaks persisted wherever I had been.

Then, a *severe* hail storm came to our village in 2017 – severe enough to be a Hurricane for 20 minutes. Blessedly, I was in the library right at the time and wondered what sound I was hearing – totally different crashing sounds from a storm I haven't heard of. When I came out, I found big trees collapsed, cars were crushed by hail and, of course, roofs were damaged, too. I had leaks everywhere again and spent a painful year on my roof reconstruction by association. I had to stay in a motel twice in the middle of winter for their construction: two weeks for each stay. They removed the old ceiling before winter and reconstructed a new one in May, 2018. I had to live without a ceiling over the winter in 2017: it was exceptionally freezing that year; I had the worst cold in my life during that winter.

In the spring, after they built the new ceiling in my unit, they started the roof job. They completed the job 90% and stopped the construction and came back the next day. Then, you know what happened? Suddenly it rained out of the blue and I had a good amount of water stains on my brand new ceiling again. They sealed up the new roof right next day and apparently all the roofs and ceilings are fine after that. I don't know why, but roof leaks had harassed me aggressively for more than two decades. In a way, I am glad that I live in a small condo now. **When we live in bigger houses, we can go through hellish lives for all sorts of repairs.** These are a few of the problems I run into since I have lived in a small condo. My recommendation is buying a newish small condo. Not only money, it can save you a lot of headaches.

* * *

Summary

1. Do not make others jealous, especially when you do not have enough money yourself.
2. People can end up paying double the amount of houses with mortgages – getting no profit out of vanity.
3. Smaller houses are better for peace of mind.

37

Not Fighting Against Platforms

We may need to exit where we are only not to lose.
-Brad Kong

I think it is important to forget everything occasionally - **do not trust anyone, including your parents, people or religion.** I can be the only one who I can truly rely on. Lately, I found out that carbohydrates are the one causing diabetes and subsequent kidney malfunction in our bodies. I have believed that rice, which is a carbohydrate den, is the healthiest food in the world for decades as most Koreans do. I believe some get broke since they fail to accept new info. Now Israelis and Palestinians are fighting over useless lands for the name of religion. It is important to see if we are in a system putting us in the wrong direction or utilizing us in a malicious way.

I guess some people, including Italians, are smart at doing business. I saw a restaurant named Rosario the other day and noticed the owner is clever. First of all, he built a new property to found the pizzeria; he may have to pay a mortgage for it, but it may be better than paying rent forever; they will own it outright someday. Secondly, I saw they divided its space in half and made some part (about 30% of the building) for a casino slot machine cafe, which is getting popular in IL. I never go to those, so I am not sure how they make profit out of it, but I feel it would be an additional income for the restaurant. Thirdly, I saw that they made the front part of the gambling cafe for an ice cream parlor (Gelato) neatly. So this is how they set up the entire floor: pizzeria (50%), gaming cafe (30%) and ice cream shop (20%).

There was a Chinese restaurant near my home that closed out permanently last year; they expanded *rental* space double pointlessly in the end. It was a take-out place originally, but renting an extra space and remodeling it to a luxury dining area didn't bring them any profit – especially after Covid. **When it comes to an offline business, rent can be the killer, according to my experience** (the same as personal finance). I have a friend paying over $10,000 a month for rent for his Italian restaurante. He made great plans to have a full liquor bar with an alcohol license and join the school lunch program. I suggested ideas like having a "self-order machine" like Taco Bell, instead of hiring servers who require tips, but he didn't listen to me.

As I mentioned before, having a habit of "trying something new at least once" is important; it is ok even if it's just a new restaurant or menu; see if you can meet a new person once a month as well. I know these are all bothersome. But these can help us realize there is a *better* option. Getting stuck in a wrong destiny may not happen to young people in general. But, as we get older, we can see ourselves trying new things less every year.

* * *

The definition of *platform* is "a standard for the hardware of a computer system running softwares." What I try to mean by *it* is "a huge system trying to make money out of visitors." And the visitors can be us. Since the word originated from a train station, let's suppose that there is a station and we are the passengers on a train; millions of trains pass through the station everyday. The owner of the train station will make money whenever a train passes. Maybe he or she charges toll fees on trains; if we are on a train, basically we are the ones who pay for it; *the owner is the one making money out of us.*

I think a real example of a platform is a site like Facebook; it shows over a billion people visit Facebook everyday. Who is the one making money out of it? Zuckerberg. No visitor makes money; mostly, they just get addicted to the site and lose time and mental energy in the form of attention. He is the train station owner and employees work for him at the station. Imagine that all the visitors are the passengers on the trains; maybe these are free trains since Facebook is free upfront. However, we have to see millions of ads on the walls during the rides. Also we may have to use facilities the station provides while paying some money: snack bars; restrooms requiring coins; ATM; shopping malls or flea market stores along the aisles; news stands, magazine counters;

etc. And maybe some companies want to post ads on the wall and pay the station.

Another example of a platform could be KDP[20] at Amazon, which is the largest online bookstore selling worldwide. More smartly, the company also built a self publishing system, connecting with sales; now people can publish books easily with KDP. Authors don't have to go door to door of publishing companies, asking to publish their manuscripts any more thanks to it. Nonetheless, KDP will take out 40% of our book sale profit, whenever a book is sold. Again, millions of writers will go through a station "KDP" and it will make money out of authors. FYI, I am *not* against it. I actually appreciate Amazon since I had no idea about how to publish my book: I believe most do not know it, either.

At this angle of view, I think the biggest platform in this country is the U.S. Federal Government. People can come here legally and make money in this country. Yet we need to pay taxes if we make any money anyhow. If we cannot get a job or fail a business, it is our fault. But, if we make any gain, we have to pay tax. In case we make a huge amount of dough, we have to pay more tax at a higher rate **– it's smart as the platform owners never lose.** They may help us make as much money as possible; we just have to pay tax, accordingly. I am not against the federal government since they helped me a lot. I know the federal tax rate is higher than the States in general, but it has more deductions, too. Also, my family received

---

[20] Kindle Direct Publishing.

stimulus checks when the COVID was everywhere in 2020. I think I did my best to help society since my work, the nursing home was a health care place, too; I helped seniors for seven years, after all.

* * *

The platform I am not particularly happy about is Illinois State. It is not just me as IL loses residents every single year, according to the statistics, while the total population in the U.S. is increasing. **It is more astonishing since the housing and living costs in IL are three times cheaper than those in the east and west coastal States.** Ironically, a large portion of the residents are Latin Americans who usually give out a lot of babies. Why is depopulation happening? In my opinion, IL is stingy to residents, while trying to harvest more taxes from them than others. There are seven States not charging State income tax, as of 2023: Wyoming, Washington, Texas, South Dakota, Nevada, Florida and Alaska. The highest number of migrants move into TX these days, including the world richest man, Musk. The Tesla factory also permanently moved into Austin, TX in 2021. Florida gets tons of retirees, while IL loses them.

Not only does IL have State income tax, but it is higher[21] than many others. However, there is something I like to point out: When a State has high income tax, usually it has low property tax. Double whammy is happening in Illinois: **While it has high income tax, the property**

---

[21] 4.95% in 2023.

tax of IL is the second highest in the nation, only next to New Jersey – the 2nd highest out of 50 States. Chicagoland[22] has probably *the highest* property tax in America, where half of IL residents are living. Having two high taxes is a double blow by itself, but here is one more thing not to ignore. Is the IL reasonably generous to residents since it takes more than others? **Absolutely not.** According to my experience, all they do is take money diligently. All I have done is pay a large sum of taxes every year, whereas I have never gotten anything back in the last seventeen years: no stimulus check from the States, no unemployment benefit or any type of help, whatsoever.

I resigned from the weekend dishwashing job last year since a new company, Morrison, took over only the dining in the nursing home. I filed an application for unemployment benefits as the HR sent a letter to suggest it; the process was tedious, but they decided to give me $302 a week for 26 weeks, originally. I thought finally I got a bit of help from the State after all those taxes I have paid for two decades; the amount of State income taxes has always been much more than the federal ones for me.

But, a month later, they suddenly contacted me and said "Not being able to transfer to a new department" does not qualify for the benefits (even if it was beyond my control). I thought that, at least, they would let me keep the $1,200 they already sent by April, 2022. The situation looked like a poor dishwasher just lost a job after seven

---

[22] For example, Lake and Cook county.

years of employment due to the company outsourcing issue, which was not my fault. They answered, "No." They asked me to pay $1,200 back, so I sent a check right away. I paid $1,500 States income tax only in 2021. **They could not even let me keep the $1,200 once in my life since I lost a job?** I thought it was too much. It is an extremely stingy State – no wonder why everyone is leaving.

* * *

Another thing I do not like about IL is the tax filing site. I understand the government made a new site, so they can collect tax efficiently. Since I made some capital gains out of stock trades in 2021, I paid $250 estimated tax for the State that year. Paying an estimated tax means paying an income tax a year earlier (2021) since I may have to pay too much in 2022. You would not believe how much they tried to hide the info about my estimated tax already paid – I was not able to find it. Eventually, I did, but had to try so hard. Unless I made a separate note at home, I could have easily forgotten about it. **I almost felt like they made it that way intentionally, so they can collect more taxes, thanks to the forgetfulness of residents.** For sure, they have tried so hard not to give out a benefit even though I had a low income job.

Also, by rule, when we invest in stocks of a company headquartered in IL, we are not supposed to pay State tax on the dividend of that company; it is called "High Impact Business Program in IL" and four companies are listed in the program in 2022: Walgreen, Abbvie, Abbott Laboratory and Caterpillar. I could not believe how much the government hid the info. Type "High Impact Business IL" in Google and see what results come out; I checked that, at least, **no government related site showed the info;** they tried super hard to hide the simple listing of four companies. I sensed they want investors to pay more tax on dividends, for not being aware of it.

As a result, I seriously considered moving to Texas four years ago in 2019. I already bought my house here in 2013, so it was a hassle; all the houses in America were cheap in 2013, because of the mortgage bubble burst. **I couldn't find a condo for the similar price in the Lone Star State in 2019.** If I still lived in an APT then, I must have moved to Texas by now. I thought I would forget about State tax for good, which, unfortunately, did not work out.

Still, Illinois has some advantages over others. It has relatively sufficient public transportations, so my family has lived without a car since 2017. Also everything is cheaper than coastal areas in America. It has the top ranked public Ivy Leagues, according to the U.S. News and Report (e.g., UIUC). It has a lot of quality libraries (the 2nd highest number of libraries in the nation, next to NY). Also the weather is cool while the Earth is getting hotter, due to global warming. I am originally from Seoul, Korea and have always missed a megapolis. Chicago is the third largest in America and I have enjoyed working around, as the big city atmosphere and endless streets to walk are indispensable to me. I hope IL will get close to TX someday; there are reasons why it loses citizens constantly, while Texas gains. People are not fools and will know which one is better one way or another.

* * *

Summary

1. We have to check if the system we are in is the best, once in a while.
2. Some lose money more since the platform they are in takes more advantage of them.
3. One excellent legal way to save on tax is living in a small condo.

38

Lack of Financial Knowledge

What we do not know may kill us.
-Brad Kong

Thomas Piketty is a professor of EHESS[23] in France. He suggested a controversial theory in his book *Capital in the Twenty-First Century*: The rate of return on capital is greater than the rate of economic growth over the long term. In other words, it reads that **people will make more money out of investment than salary from work.** According to his theory, investors will get richer than ever, while those who do not invest won't get out of average lives, no matter how much they work. Personally, I have been living fully on dividend and interest income since 2022. My life is far from luxury, though; probably, the biggest lavishness I can have is dining at Thai or Indian restaurants, sometimes. Nonetheless, I feel blessed that I don't have to go to work these days.

I think we should never disregard our intuitions: This can be the most formidable weapon from our sub-consciousness. We cannot explain it visibly in a

---

[23] Economics at the School for Advanced Studies in the Social Sciences.

word, but it can be more important than simple knowledge. I think we should walk away if we do not feel good about anything: Never ignore the first impression or just a bad feeling out of nowhere. It's possible there are trillions of logic behind our gut feelings. This sixth sense can help us increase profits, avoid losses or even save our lives. While intuitions matter, knowledge is the next powerful thing for survival. A little bit of health knowledge can save us literally millions of dollars. We can get plenty of info from YouTube or Netflix as well. Knowledge and info are two major tools, which does not necessarily cost more to get.

I believe what's supreme in personal finance is getting rid of debts. I suggest people not to jump into an investment when they are not sure; I know it's extremely hard to make a profit out of it. In fact, I decided to stop buying stocks after 2021 although I will keep my current portfolio forever, which will give me about $30,000 in dividends and interest every year. There were some Korean trolls who talked about leveraged *loans*, but it seemed they never understood a simple thing: **No point to invest while we have a debt**; the chance to lose money out of debt interest is 100%; often, the amount is not that small. On the contrary, the chance to make some money out of investment is less than 30% (probably close to 0% for the trolls). It would be like going to the gym to lose weight while having a tumor – we need to extinguish fire first, before remodeling and upgrading the house.

* * *

People often make the mistake that making a lot of money is primary to stay rich, which is true, to some extent. But, if we are already in the top 10% of the wealth pyramid, not making a mistake could be more crucial as **financial mistakes are often caused by greed.** I bought a small condo in full and have a portfolio of 70 company stocks, 38 company bonds and some savings; probably I will make more money with book sales and eventually inherit a moderate fortune from my parents. In this case, not losing money could matter more. My father in Korea has been wealthy for life; as far as I know, he still owns a few condos and a commercial tall building; we estimate his net worth is over $20 M in USD though no one knows how much exactly. He is clearly self-made as he lost his parents when he was a child. Here is one thing he has always made sure for me and my brother: *No debt.*

From the start, what he means by "debt" is "business debt"; he does not mean a mortgage, car loan or other consumption related debts. Buying a house or car with debt has been out of his concern; I remember he always bought those with cash. I know there was a Korean troll borrowing a chunk of money for his house (mortgage) to live luxuriously to show off; he said he bought a $4 M house with a huge home loan in 2022. I am afraid my dad may look at him like an animal. Technically, there is nothing wrong with borrowing money for houses since they are naturally expensive. I think I started hating mortgage payers only because of some Korean troll; especially, one always showed off as nasty as possible, even though all he had was diverse debts.

The first real finance I read was *Rich Dad Poor Dad* by Kyosaki in 2007. Then, my wife strongly suggested it when we were at the Borders one day. I was not interested in the beginning, so she started to read the prologue to me. By the time she finished the first paragraph, I decided to buy it. I think I ordered a used copy online, though. Here are the key points I understood: **An asset is something putting money in our pockets**; bank interest can be an example, which we get automatically only because we have some money in the bank. If we can live only on interests without touching the original capital, our wealth can last forever.

This actually has been a key principle for me in the last fifteen years. When we have a small amount of money, it may not make a noticeable difference. Yet suppose we have $1,000,000 in AT&T stock. I know it's a fortune, but more people than we evaluate may have it. The stock gives 6% dividend a year, just like bank interest – which means we can get a $60,000 dividend a year, automatically. **If we can live on less than that $60,000 every year, the $1,000,000 will last forever.** A good amount of our population has more than $1 M these days. This is why there are people living without a job everywhere; honestly, this includes me, even though I am getting only $30,000 a year from my portfolio.

I had a chance to get some money from my parents after my daughter was born. I put all the $90,000 in my bank CDs in 2011 and started getting 3% interest a year, then. It was a nice side income as I had struggled with my business at that time. Then, suddenly the mortgage bubble burst and all the house prices dropped crazily. I was able to buy my condo for $60,000 cash, which has tripled in the past ten years. Without the concept of asset, I would have not known what to do with that $90,000, to begin with. Maybe I would have bought a racing car since holding cash has no point? What if I lost it at the casino, while trying to make it double? Thanks to the $10 used book, I gained the concept and kept accumulating money in CDs, stocks and bonds for interest and dividends since 2011. I can see that the book is still a top seller at Amazon and probably has helped tons of people not lose their capitals. While we don't get along perfectly, I appreciate my wife who introduced it to me.

* * *

Summary

1. Financial instinct and knowledge are both important.
2. Not having a debt is the prime.
3. Reading one used book helped me greatly.

39

Expensive Hobbies

Luxury was created to keep us poor.
-Brad Kong

I think writing is a hobby to help us survive through a recession. COVID pandemic is not completely over yet, as of 2023; Google laid off 12,000 employees this year; some economists expect us to get into depression slowly. I quit my job last year and live without a car now. You know the cruel Chicago winter; everyone needs to be locked inside for the next five months: *What can I do during a few years of a financial ice age coming?* While most hobbies cost money, I don't think writing does; it helped me kill some time and save money; in the best case, my books sell, too. I have already published dozens of books and the number in the library will increase. Besides, I don't think it's psychologically healthy that we cannot express what we want to say and bite our tongues – alternatively, we can do it in writing, instead of saying.

Sometimes, I wonder why I have kept writing; I have written millions of articles on diverse websites all over for the past two decades. I had conflicts with internet trolls, but I couldn't stop writing. There was one time an offended loser called a fire truck to my business as revenge in 2009; police said someone made a prank call to 911 and falsely reported that there was an oven fire in my game store. Maybe I am lonely as I do not have many friends; I may be addicted to the internet. Or maybe I do not want to let good ideas slip away into oblivion. **Regardless, I think that it is good to keep writing as a hobby**; it can be better than riding a motorbike, which can be fatal.

In my personal finance, writing is profitable *even if* it does not bring any income. I have savings and could have lost a lot if I have different hobbies. Being obsessed with writing prevents me from visiting an exotic motor dealership or casino. Some lose fortunes since they are into cash-burning hobbies: audio equipment upgrading, DSLR photography, yacht fishing, safari hunting, etc. It would be great if my books sell, though.

* * *

What would you believe makes a person decent? These were moments when I felt some people are respectable:

- When a rich person still eat at modest restaurants (Hartono,Buffet, etc)
- When a super rich lives without a car (Chow Yun-fat, Kotegawa, etc)
- Minimalists
- When a rich still works a little (e.g. writing)
- When a person has a easier job
- When a person does not eat or talk much

- When a person still read a lot amid having a fortune (Berggruen, Gates, etc)
- When a person completely owns a house without a loan (25% of Americans)
- When a wealthy live in a smaller condo
- When a person marries only once and has a child

In my opinion, when a person is missing out on having a child, he or she may not understand half of the social phenomena; they may not understand how the world works; singles may be crippled in getting full experiences. At the same time, I believe it is also pointless to go crazy for more children since overpopulation is coming closer. To me, the father of *one child* can be a winner in the modern day's marriage system – half single and married. I think I have felt attraction from people living plainly while having enough money; they do not show off, but spend money if necessary without desperation; **I believe that is where *decency* comes from.** Both being greedy or suffering financially *never* look good; some get poorer from the point since they will push out appeals farther.

I observed that some ended up broke because they waste all their passion and talents only on hobbies or other things; they fail to connect their flairs with opportunities to make money productively. Unless their hobbies bring them a profit, they tend to be impoverished forever. An example is me, unfortunately. When I think about it now, I have written zillions of articles on myriads of sites for nothing in the last 23 years – no one paid, rewarded or appreciated me for this. It brought me a little bit of fame only online since some remember my pen name. I realize too late that I have so much passion for writing; I just wasted a chunk of my lifetime only because I did not know anything about self-publishing. All I heard was some rejection stories of known writers – Harry Potter was rejected forty times or something like that.

To make things worse, I often made a lot of enemies, instead of friends since I didn't forgive nasty trolls all the time; I often attacked them back. As a result, I have wasted the first forty years of my life for nothing in writing. However, I may be lucky as I still may have 50 years left if I die at 100. Some really waste their whole life for various reasons. I guess I can publish 600 books before I die if I can write one book a month from now. Have you heard of "Ferrari beggars" in Japan? There is a group of people spending all their salaries on Ferrari cars in the country. Alternatively, I think they could have used their passion to work for Ferrari dealerships or similar; I am pretty sure they could have used their knowledge. Suppose there is a girl who likes to dance. She can waste her rage to dance at a nightclub. Or she can use it to work as an instructor at a dancing school. In general, losers tend to waste time, and never use energy in a constructive way.

* * *

After quitting my job in 2022, writing has been my sole profession. So I wondered how I could increase my book sales to support my family. I cannot imagine how Melville would have felt since he had four kids by the time he started writing *Moby-Dick*; I had no clue how Dickens took care of his family, including 10 children; Before that, I don't think I can even produce that many, to begin with. I feel lucky that I have only one child; I feel even luckier that the earth is overcrowded with 8 billion people, so I don't have to pressure myself to produce more offspring. I have a little income from investment and savings, but writing is supposed to be my major source from now. Here are 4 things I decided to try to increase sales after analyzing top sellers, which I hope will be helpful in case you write for a side.

First of all, I concluded that I need to write as many pages as possible to increase sales. I originally planned to write 300 pages for the final book, but increased my target to 700 pages. This is merely psychology – when readers buy a book, they prefer thicker ones for similar prices. It is natural to go for *more* for the same money. I noticed that most bestsellers are at least 400 pages and *Life force* by Robinson is even 720 pages. My wife reads a lot by Grisham and Patterson and these are up to 600 pages, proving readers prefer thicker ones. It shows Alchemist by Coelho eventually sold over 150 million copies. He confessed that only two copies were sold in the first six months after release in 1985, which was only 170 pages. It was the second book for Coelho, so he must be nameless then. Not many buy a thin one from an unknown writer. *The Old Man and the Sea* by Hemingway has sold millions of copies, even though it is 120 pages, but it won the Nobel Prize in 1954. I am talking about strategies for ordinary writers like me.

Another advantage for a thick book is extra library purchases in my opinion. When patrons borrow thick books, it usually takes longer for them to return them. So it's possible there are more waiting for those. It is possible for a library to buy an extra copy of it since there are too many bookworms waiting. America has 140,000 libraries. If one library buys an extra copy, it's extra sales of 100,000 books for authors. KDP shows that I can make about $7 profit whenever my final book sells. Then, it could be $700,000 extra profit. Less likely that is going to happen, but it is possible I can sell 2,000 books, instead of 1,000, by writing a thicker one.

Secondly, I guess my books need to be written in English to sell more, while Korean is easier for me. This must be no problem for Americans, though many reading this book are non-English speakers, according to the KDP report. I did not realize the Korean population is only 0.05% of the world as I mistakenly believed it is 5%. Only the USA population is 6 times bigger than that of South Korea. And there are 67 countries whose primary language is English, including the UK, Canada, Australia, New Zealand, Singapore, South Africa, etc. Also some like India or China have the largest populations, who know how to read English. Nevertheless, there are popular authors having sold over 1 million copies only in Korea. Again, I am talking about plans for the average Joes.

Thirdly, **I think it's advantageous to include certain numbers in titles, especially for**

non-fictions – How many points will the author cover in his book? I know it since I have posted countless articles online; the numbers in titles attracted more clicks. "10 Reasons Why" in this book is good. Some all-time bestsellers on Amazon are *The 48 Laws of Power*, *12 Rules for Life* and *The 7 Habits of Highly Effective People*. It seems numbers make readers curious; they love to know contents included in the numbers. I like Dobelli, but his book *Art of thinking clearly* wasn't a hit. If he wrote the title as "99 ways to think clearly," which was the contents, the sales could have been much better.

Lastly, I think uniqueness matters. I hope this book will be a success. Also I like to hear readers say, "I have never seen a book like this." There are over 2 million new titles published only in America every year. But I feel like too many books have contents that I have seen somewhere else before. Most do not include unique ideas or experience, not to mention style. For example, I think *Art of Thinking clearly* by Dobelli failed because it does not have much unique personal experience. It includes only theories and experiments from other books. Simply, the author read a lot and collected info in line – none of his own ideas. Any book can be boring without distinctive stories, so I could not finish it the past six months. We ought to put peculiarities and honesty to make a book vivid.

I see a lot of books written in a rushed way, many of which are less than 250 pages. Maybe they have jobs other than writing or do not have much savings to win some time to write slowly. I feel lucky in that sense, while I feel sorry for them, too. Coco Chanel once said, "The best things in life are free." Writing may not be exactly free, but it is a hobby to relieve our stresses and arrange our thoughts. When I say what I really want to say, it comforts my rage a little bit. And, sometimes, we can get some money and fame that way, too.

* * *

Currently, my favorite hobbies are walking, riding a scooter and reading books, all of which don't cost a lot. I try to walk for a long distance one day a week and the total distance has been up to 30 miles a day, sometimes. I usually walk to the bus hub behind the mall, which is three miles away from my home. There used to be a local bus to get there every hour, but the village canceled it after COVID came in 2020. I hope they will reschedule it soon, but now I just have to walk or ride a scooter to get to the terminal hub. Once I get there, it has millions of buses going everywhere in Chicagoland. Probably, it has 15 gates for buses with different routes while many of them go to downtown Chicago one way or another.

I got the long distance walking habit when I was a teenager thanks to my brother, who used to walk surprisingly long distances. He made me realize that a human can walk that long. I think Seoul is different from any cities I've seen in America and it is designed ideally for walking. The population of the capital, including the vicinity, is almost 25 millions and the entire area is packed with 300 subway stations and myriads of bus lines; the city is hell for drivers, but heaven for walkers. The streets in Seoul are somewhat like never-ending shopping malls – endless miles of coffee shops, restaurants, stores, entertainments, etc. If we can combine 1,000 shopping malls in America and align them in line, it could be the countless streets in Seoul – a stroller's paradise. The streets with shops – we can walk the whole week and these will never end. In fact, I had strolled for two decades like a mad man, yet I was not able to cover half of the city. When we check the streets of Seoul on YouTube, we can see that citizens are overall skinny. Trust me that it's not because of their food – they just walk a lot. Plus, it has the world's cleanest public transportations. My wife said it is ten times more decent than that of Chicago. Plus, the weather is mild, so wandering has always been pleasant.

On the contrary, I do not see any long enough streets in an American city. According to my experience, the longest fun street on the west coast was Hollywood Boulevard in LA, having Mann's Chinese Theater. I have been there probably three times since my brother used to live in San Diego. It was long, but I recall that just six hours were enough to cover it all. Downtown San Diego was nice, but I think three days were enough to go everywhere. In the Midwest, Downtown Dells, WI was similar to the Niagara falls, including the "Ripley's Believe It or Not! museum," but the *walking everywhere* was over in just three hours. I read one Norwegian guy visited Seoul 18 times only to walk around on the streets – healthy joy for residents without costing much.

Depending on the situation, a hobby can cost a fortune. I saw a sports car accident on the news the other day. The driver must have blown $240,000 in the air for nothing and got a criminal record. We can live like that or we do not have to. Bond prices have dropped significantly since 2022. A lot of my CDs are getting matured and I will have a small fortune in my hands soon. Personally, I plan to put all of it in bond ETFs as *getting more interest* brings me *pleasure*. Do you know who else got the same feeling? John D. Rockefeller; he said exactly the same thing 200 years ago. I guess history will keep repeating now.

* * *

Summary

1. We don't need to have an expensive hobby.
2. Some recreations don't cost money.
3. Some people even make money out of their hobbies.

40

Not Doing Things Yourself

If you cannot repair it, see if you can live without it.
-Brad Kong

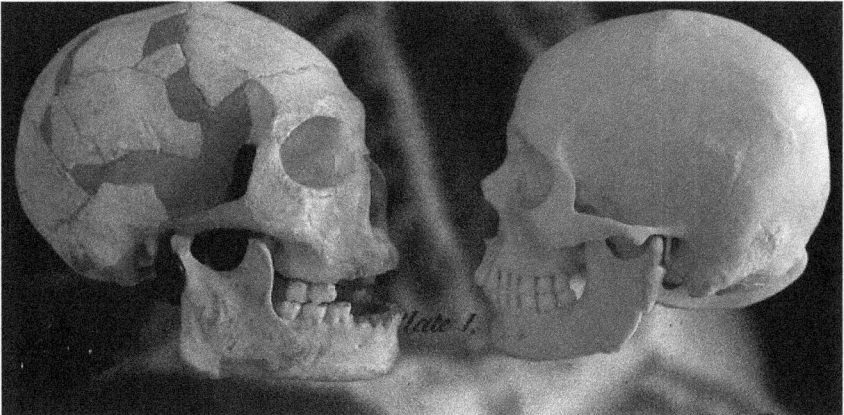

In *Sapiens,* Harari argued that the human brain has actually decreased in the last 200,000 years since the age of foraging. He explains that our ancestors needed to do everything *well* only to survive then. People don't know how to do many things these days – as a result, no one can survive in the mountains just for one night during the winter. There are people calling for a professional for every issue. The problem is, unfortunately, not every business they call is really professional; many of them are deceptive, too. I saw a couple of TV programs regarding this matter. They showed how some HVAC[24] or garage door technicians deceive customers. One way not to become a victim of frauds can be living without a lot of stuff in my opinion. For instance, I do not own a garage since I live in a condo, so garage door deception will never ever happen to me. Incidentally, I don't own a car, either; the biggest reason why I abandoned the ownership was I had decades of bad experiences with auto mechanics, including "no work done" with overcharges.

In *12 Rules for Life*, Peterson mentioned that "Achieving a hard goal is more related to personality and growth than making money." I agree since I can see that some people are still cheesy despite their money. I concluded that decency is not automatically from owning currencies, while they help people get it. As I have saved more as I get older, I find myself to be more interested in personal quality, which I didn't care about before. I don't want to give bad feelings to others by overspending my own money, which is a loss, after all; I prefer to be remembered amiable to others.

Sometimes, I truly wonder where my strong desire to write comes from. I assume virtually everyone has a desire to leave something before dying; that's why some women are obsessed with updating photos on Instagram, which is a little superficial. People with deep minds want to leave records from their mental works. One of the most efficient ways to record analyses is writing. I think that is

---

[24] heating, ventilation and air conditioning.

the reason why I prefer writing, instead of putting my face online, which will protect me in the end. Regardless, I noticed that self-publishing itself is getting more popular in general.

I don't think being successful in finance is about living diligently – we don't have to be busy to be rich. I believe success is more related to reducing the time we waste, which can be achieved by making our lives more efficient overall. When I was at the Forest park station the other day (the last stop of the blue line subway), I saw several people hanging around for no apparent reason. I didn't know what they wanted, but they made people waiting very uncomfortable. I was dying to get on my bus before anyone addressed me. Security cameras were everywhere, but they were smoking in and out of the terminal and approaching people groundlessly, while making them feel awkward.

* * *

Repairing things ourselves can give us a reasonable challenge; we may learn new skills and can grow ourselves little after a project. Hiring others is getting more expensive these days, which won't be reversible. With the help of YouTube, Home Depot, Autozone, etc, we can do things ourselves now. Doing it on our own has at least three practical advantages in my opinion. First of all, we can save money, of course.

Secondly, we may face some obstacles and start using parts of our brains we have never used. It's proven that human bodies can turn on different genes we have never used before, depending on conditions. I guess challenges can help brain development or dementia prevention in similar ways. I tried knitting next to my wife before. Conclusively, I got frustrated and gave up. I tried to figure out how it works, but I was not able to knit even a simple thing. Even my daughter, who was nine then, did a better job than me. It was a challenge I have never had in the past five decades, and I found a different type of intelligence might be needed. We are familiar only with what we have done and have lost the capability to triumph new things. We can realize what skill we are missing, which can increase our survival rate in the end.

Thirdly, in the opposite way, we can run into some unexpected talents we did not notice we have. For example, I did not know I had a huge desire to write before publishing a book in 2022. Before then, writing addiction has been a problem for me, which had me wasting ten hours a day on browsing and writing on sites for long. In fact, it was worse than waste since I made a lot of enemies along the way. My pointless browsing gradually disappeared after starting writing a real book series. Now I am spending hours a day on writing my own books without checking the internet much. I think it's more productive since browsing used to make my brain hurt. The best part of doing things on our own is finding something new in ourselves.

These are examples of the things I have done on my own for years, instead of hiring others.

1. I have always filed taxes myself in the last 24 years. Recently, I started using "freetaxusa.com" and I am happy with it. It should be perfectly free unless you have a huge income to report. Before using it, I made a mistake, so I did not get a $1,000 annual credit for my child for many years. The first year I used it was 2019 when I got a $1,000 direct deposit for the first time. For IL State tax, I just use this government site[25], which is not perfect, but fine since it's totally free. I heard that H&R Block can charge us $200 for a simple filing, which can end up as a $10,000 fee for the next 50 years.

2. I did some plumbing work in my condo myself: new bathtub wall construction; kitchen and bathroom faucet changes; etc. I was able to do these with help from Youtube videos, Home depot, Ace Hardware and Enterprise rental cars nearby. I had to rent a van only for one day to bring Durock wall supplies, which cost me $50 in 2019. I learned new skills along the way.

3. I used to change the air filters, spark plugs and engine oil of a car myself.

---

[25] https://mytax.illinois.gov

4. I have *self*-published 34 books since 2022. I have done editing with help of Google Doc. I have designed book covers with Edit.org, which costs me $69 a year; I publish with KDP of Amazon. Then, I do marketing with social media, including Reddit and Instagram. If I hire people for all those, it could have cost $10,000 or more. The worst part is the final products could have been something I did not expect. I am the most enthusiastic reader of my own books and try to make products I like to buy.

5. While I owned the video game store, I had not been able to hire anyone. Basically, I did everything myself starting from cleaning the carpet (I hired Miguel for window washing, though). I was an online sales agent and a security guard there as well. I did everything although my wife helped me occasionally, which I *appreciate*.

6. I have never hired a financial advisor for my investment in the last decade. I started stock investing in 2011; I have done fine and even made a small fortune in 2021. **I don't think hiring a professional guarantees anything, especially in stock trading.** In fact, it is possible I could have lost money since I had been in loss on PBI stock for years. I just did not sell it until January 2022 and made $20,000 profit out of selling all my PBI shares one day. **In this case, actually hiring "pro" could have hurt long term profits.** It is possible that an advisor could have pushed me to sell earlier.

Then, I could have lost double – the financial advisor fee and stock loss.

7. My wife teaches how to play the violin to my daughter everyday. She usually charges up to $100 an hour since she has a doctorate degree in violin.

My biggest fear is to become a person who doesn't know how to do anything except getting dividends out of portfolio. I guess we need to attempt new things once in a while.

* * *

Summary

1. We can save money by *doing things on our own*.
2. It can bring us a new opportunity by trying something new.
3. It can help us find new talents we didn't know we have.

Author's Note

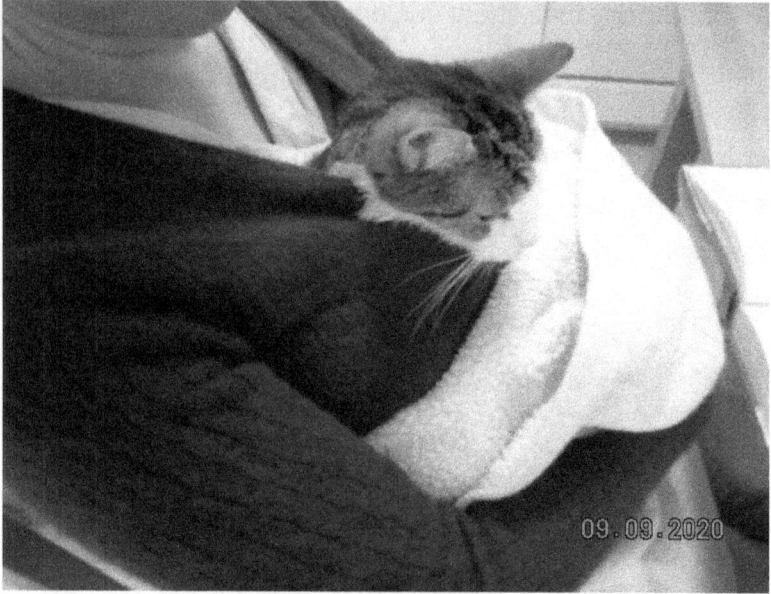

Congratulations: I truly appreciate you finishing my book until the end. The cat in the photo is Yang (Oscar) who I mentioned in Chapter 30 of *UnBrokable* III*; it was taken only a few days before he passed away. We had cherishable memories, but he couldn't get over the blood cancer in the end.

I was born and raised in South Korea and immigrated to America in my 20s; that was 24 years ago since it's 2023 now. In the beginning, I failed getting accepted to prestigious Ivy league schools although SUNYat Buffalo is great. Then I graduated from college with a 2.6 GPA by 2005, so I decided not to go to graduate school. Instead, I started my own business, but it wasn't very successful for 8 years. Subsequently, my career at the nursing home also didn't work out as I planned even though I won two certificates during the 7 years; now I try to be a writer.

If you believe this book can be helpful to others and have a minute to spare, ***I would appreciate a rating;*** *I do read all the reviews myself and use them to improve writing.* Reviews from readers like you make a difference; please let me know what you think. I sincerely wish my best luck to you!

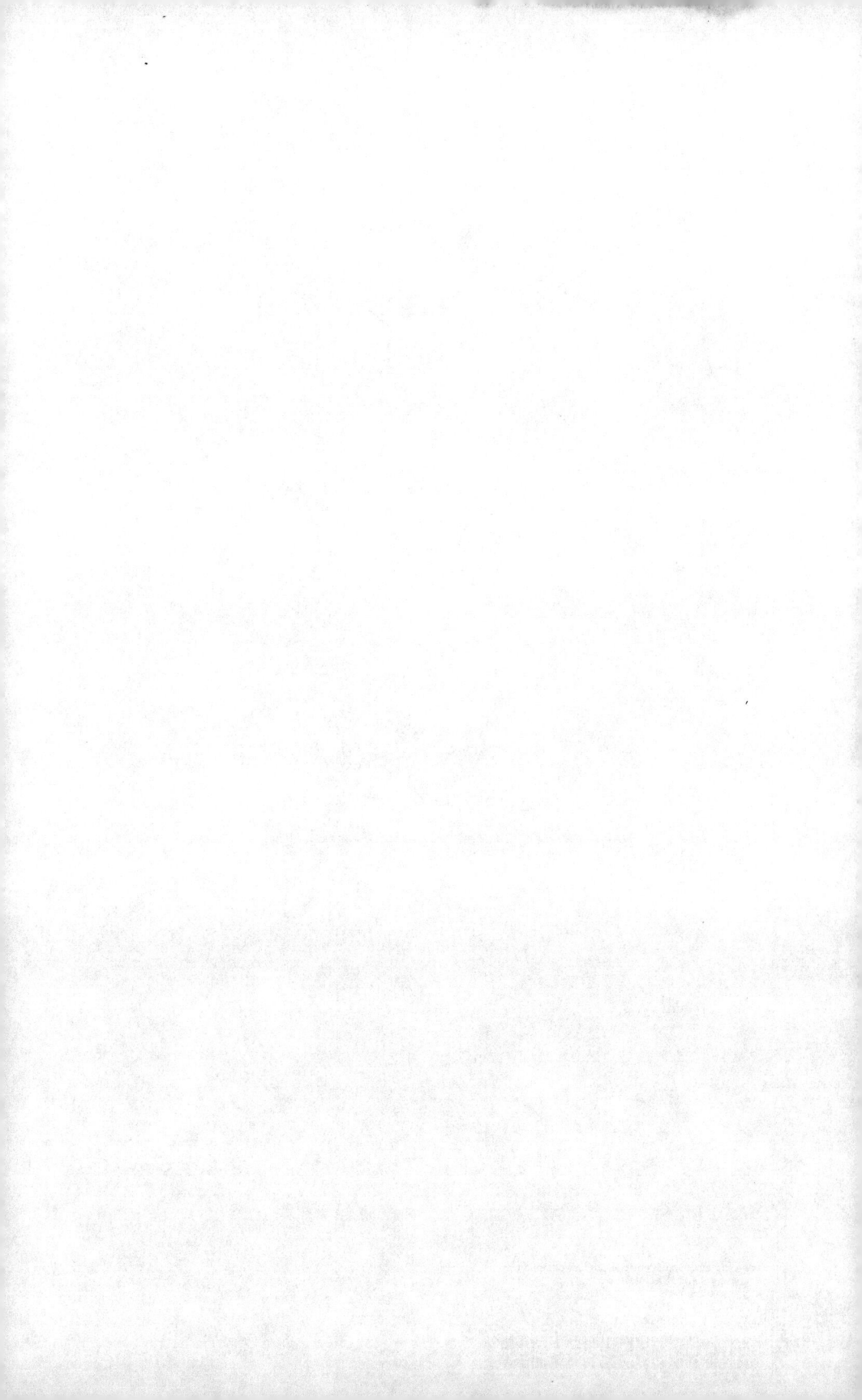

www.ingramcontent.com/pod-product-compliance
Lightning Source LLC
Chambersburg PA
CBHW021132020426
42331CB00005B/734